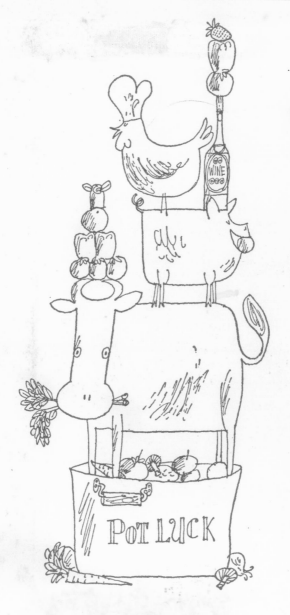

POT LUCK

Helen Corbitt's

POTLUCK

ALSO BY HELEN CORBITT

Helen Corbitt's Cookbook

Helen Corbitt's
POTLUCK

BY HELEN CORBITT
DIRECTOR OF RESTAURANTS
AT NEIMAN-MARCUS

HOUGHTON MIFFLIN COMPANY

BOSTON

Dedicated to
MY PUBLISHERS
Men of Strong Wills and Great Patience

Contents

Introduction

WHY call this book *Potluck?* Mostly because over the years my name has been associated with Potluck. Wherever I have been Potluck has become the most popular item on the menu, even among the sophisticated customers in the Zodiac Room at Neiman-Marcus. This book is designed to encourage an intelligent attitude toward leftovers and an experimental utilization of a whole raft of ideas. At Neiman-Marcus our menu lists a Potluck luncheon and our men guests say "it is just like going home for lunch." Our women guests confess they get wonderful inspirations from Potluck luncheons (if they can guess the ingredients). I happen to think that restaurant food should do just that — make the men feel comfortably at home and give the women notions of new dishes they can create in their own kitchens.

Potluck does not mean always the using up of leftovers. It is, rather, what you decide to have for lunch or dinner *today,* from things on hand, in the refrigerator, the pantry, or in your Christmas basket. If you have developed a kindly attitude toward your fellowman, and have a reasonable delight in discovering new tastes to surprise and please him, you will make Potluck pleasant to come home to.

All of us are cooks — some of us one night a week, some seven days a week and three times a day. Some of us like to cook and brag about our culinary accomplishments. Some of us enjoy bewailing our lot, but all of us will admit we like the appreciation of those who sit down to share the results.

With informal living outpacing itself, more and more homemakers and hostesses are turning to casserole and skillet cooking and serving. They may be decorative or they may be prosaic, but their charm lies in the ease with which they allow a hostess to command any situation.

This is a collection of Potlucks I like to serve. They do not take too much time or effort. I think they have a versatility you might enjoy. After all you can take any recipe and add your own unique touches to make it different, if you want to. You can do anything if you really want to. How delectable and exciting is the food on your table? It is simply up to you.

If you are calorie watching, substitute, but do not expect any recipe to be as good as when made with butter and cream. You will be amazed how good you can make this substitution if you use your imagination with seasonings, wine, herbs and some positive thinking.

A thank you to friends who encourage this Potluck approach to eating, and to my many loyal employees who enjoy being different too.

HELEN CORBITT

Soups

I always like the combination of flavors and textures in soup. This is one of my favorites for Sunday night entertaining.

Bisque of Corn and Crabmeat

(FOR TEN OR TWELVE)

¼ cup chopped onion
¼ cup butter
2 tablespoons flour
½ teaspoon curry powder
4 cups fresh or frozen corn (uncooked)
4 cups milk
1 cup cream
Salt and pepper
1 pound crabmeat (I prefer lump)

Sauté the onion in the butter until soft. Add the flour and curry and cook 1 minute. Add corn chopped or put in electric blender. Cook for 5 minutes. Add milk and cream, salt and pepper and bring to a boil. Stir in the crabmeat and serve at once from the pot.

I like to serve warm corn beef sandwiches made on thin slices of buttered French bread and hot applesauce flavored with a goodly amount of horseradish with this. For dessert? Irish coffee.

A really pretty soup to whip up in a hurry for guests to sit down to is:

Tomato and Chive Soup

(FOR FOUR OR SIX)

2 cups canned tomatoes	1 stalk celery, chopped
1 tablespoon diced onion	Sour cream
	Chopped chives

Bring first three ingredients to a boil. Strain and chill. Mix with equal parts of sour cream, and add chopped chives as you serve very cold. Vary it by adding melon balls and thin strips of ham. Really in a hurry — put in the blender uncooked. Nice with a Swiss Cheese Soufflé with sautéed mushrooms, sliced thin, laid on the bottom of the soufflé dish before baking — and freshly cooked or frozen asparagus dressed with fresh lime in the barely melted butter you should pour over just before serving.

For dessert chilled fresh sugared strawberries with a rum-flavored custard to pour over.

Gumbo is as southern as fried chicken, and you may go any route you like, chicken, sea food, ham, vegetable or leftovers. Use it as a soup or a main dish.

Chicken Gumbo

(FOR EIGHT OR TEN)

½ cup chopped onion
½ cup green pepper slivered
1 cup chopped celery
Butter or salad oil
3 cups chicken broth
2 cups canned or peeled fresh tomatoes
1 bay leaf

¼ teaspoon thyme
1 cup sliced okra, fresh frozen or canned
2 tablespoons chopped parsley
¼ teaspoon Tabasco
½ teaspoon gumbo filé (you may omit)
Salt to taste

3 cups chicken pieces (or less)

Sauté the onion, green pepper and celery until soft in very little butter or salad oil. Add the rest of the ingredients except chicken and simmer for 30 minutes; add chicken and heat thoroughly. Season to your taste.

If you freeze the gumbo for future use, and like the flavor of filé, add when you reheat. Vary it also by adding whole cooked shrimp or pieces of ham or both. Serve as a main course on hot rice. Always serve with a slice of lemon whether used as soup or an entrée. One needs only a salad and perhaps a bowl of fruit for a satisfying meal.

P.S. Dip green pepper in boiling water for one minute before cutting. It cuts more easily and the unpleasant oily taste that many object to is lessened.

5

I can think of nothing better to soothe one's nerves than

Zuppa Pavese

(FOR FOUR)

4 slices bread	2 cans chicken
2 tablespoons butter	consommé
4 eggs	
½ cup grated Parmesan cheese	

Trim the crusts from the bread and cut into round shape with a cooky cutter. Sauté in the butter until brown on both sides. Soft-poach the eggs in salted water. Place the eggs on the toast, and pour the hot consommé over and ladle the cheese over all.

What a nice dish to come home to after a cocktail party or after the theater or opera.

Likewise

Lemon Rice Soup

(FOR EIGHT)

1 egg yolk	4 cups (about 2 cans)
1 tablespoon lemon	chicken consommé
juice	¾ cup cooked rice
4 tablespoons Parmesan cheese	

Mix egg yolk, lemon juice and cheese. Fork-stir into boiling chicken consommé. Add rice and serve. Nice with a variety of thin bread sandwiches.

Both these soups are Italian in origin and fast becoming standbys on my list for a quick refreshment.

Cold Curried Crabmeat Soup Indienne

1 tablespoon chopped chives or green onion tops

2 tablespoons butter

2 teaspoons curry powder

2 tablespoons flour

3 cups milk

2 cups crabmeat, fresh, frozen or canned, cut in small pieces

¼ cup sherry

2 cups light cream

Sauté the chives in the butter for 1 minute. Add the curry powder and flour and cook until well blended. Add the milk and cook until thick. Heat the crabmeat in the sherry, add the cream and bring to a boil. Add to the curry mixture and cool. Serve very cold surrounded by ice, for informal entertaining.

The flavor is best if it is made the day before. With thin cucumber sandwiches and fresh pineapple fingers sprinkled with brown sugar for dessert, you have a delightful luncheon. Change in the weather? Reheat it — and change the cucumbers to very thin ham.

7

A taste treat from Spain has many interpretations.

Gazpacho

4 large ripe tomatoes, peeled
½ cucumber, peeled
¼ cup chopped green pepper
A dash of Tabasco
4 tablespoons olive oil
4 teaspoons wine vinegar
1 cup tomato juice
½ teaspoon salt
1 teaspoon grated onion
Fresh-ground pepper

Chop the tomatoes and cucumber fine, and add rest of ingredients. Strain through a sieve and chill, or put everything in an electric blender. Serve with an ice cube floating in the center of the chilled cup. Pass a tray containing a bowl of chopped cucumbers, a bowl of chopped tomatoes, tiny croutons, and one of chopped chives or parsley for each to add their own, and a bowl of sour cream would not be amiss.

Served in ceramic tomatoes it is a beautiful first course — and did you ever stop to think that both children and adults might like any soup, even canned, served in containers such as these? Serve in a punch bowl for a buffet or for an added touch at a cocktail party. It would be a nice beginning for a dinner with a Roasted Beef Brisket, Garlic Grits and your favorite green vegetable.

Garlic Grits

2 cups grits   1½ quarts warter

Cook together until done. Add:

½ cup milk   ¼ pound (1 stick)
 2 rolls garlic cheese   butter
 4 eggs beaten   Salt and pepper to taste

Pour into a buttered casserole. Sprinkle with Parmesan cheese and paprika. Bake at 300° for 30 minutes. For dessert — an Apple Compote.

Cold Avocado Soup is beautiful to look at and to taste. I serve it in a ceramic tulip cup. I also serve canned jellied madrilène with avocado mashed with lime on top, and canned jellied chicken consommé with halves of white grapes and sometimes strips of ham on top. All pretty, all Potlucks! Especially in the tulip cup.

Avocado Soup

(FOR EIGHT OR TEN)

4 tablespoons butter	¼ teaspoon powdered
4 tablespoons flour	ginger (you may
2 cups milk	omit)
2 cups cream	Grated rind of 1 orange
3 avocados	Salt to taste

Melt butter, add flour. Cook until bubbly. Add milk and cream. Cook until thickened and smooth. Cool. Peel and mash avocados. Add to the cream sauce with the ginger and orange rind. Put in electric blender until smooth as velvet. Chill. Serve very cold with diced avocado on top, and whipped cream if you like and grated orange peel.

I use this for a luncheon soup, with a good big spoonful of chicken salad nested in fresh fruit. Especially nice for spring and summer. You only need two courses. I slice cinnamon bread paper thin and oven brown to serve with both. You may buy cinnamon bread or make it. Spread your rolled out dough with butter, and half sugar and cinnamon. Roll up like a jelly roll, and bake. This makes a pretty tea sandwich bread also.

10

This soup will impress someone, and for yogurt admirers it will soothe even the particular! Persian in origin.

Cold Yogurt Soup

½ cup raisins
3 cups yogurt
½ cup coffee cream
1 hard-cooked egg
6 ice cubes
½ cup finely chopped cucumber

¼ cup finely chopped green onion
1 teaspoon salt
½ teaspoon pepper
1 cup cold water
1 tablespoon chopped parsley

1 tablespoon chopped fresh dill
(or 1 teaspoon dried)

Soak raisins in cold water. Put yogurt in mixing bowl with the cream, egg, ice cubes, cucumber, onion, salt and pepper. Stir well. Add the drained raisins and cold water. Refrigerate for several hours. Serve with chopped parsley and dill. Try serving it at a cocktail party sometime.

Poultry

There are many reasons why chicken should play a big part in menu planning. Moderate in calories, modest in price, inexhaustible in ways of preparation — what more can you ask for except some new variation in preparation? Everyone has a freezing compartment today, and if you want to be prepared, you probably would have a few chicken breasts on hand for the unexpected guest. The results of these two recipes are not unexpected.

Curry of Chicken Breasts

(FOR FOUR)

2 tablespoons chopped onion

2 tablespoons chopped celery (may be omitted)

3 tablespoons butter

¼ teaspoon salt

2 teaspoons curry powder

3 tablespoons flour

1 cup milk (or half milk, half chicken stock)

½ cup cream

1 tablespoon sherry (may be omitted)

¼ cup diced pickled peaches

4 6- to 8-ounce chicken breasts

1 cup chicken consommé

Croutons (you may buy them all prepared if you wish)

Parmesan cheese

Sauté onions and celery in the butter until onions are yellow; add salt and curry powder and mix thoroughly; add flour and cook until bubbly. Add milk and cream, stirring briskly until smooth and thick, and cook until all the starchy flavor has disappeared. Add sherry and fruit.

Poach the chicken breasts in chicken broth or water. Add to the curry sauce and simmer for 10 minutes. Spoon over the croutons, sprinkled with Parmesan cheese. This is a nice change from rice, and the texture delightful. A tray of sliced fresh fruits in place of a salad and for dessert —

French Chocolate Pie

2 egg whites
⅛ teaspoon salt
⅛ teaspoon cream of tartar
½ cup sugar
½ cup finely chopped walnuts or pecans

½ teaspoon vanilla extract
1 package (¼ pound) sweet cooking chocolate
3 tablespoons water
1 tablespoon brandy

1 cup heavy cream

Combine egg whites, salt and cream of tartar in mixing bowl. Beat until foamy throughout. Add sugar, two tablespoons at a time, beating after each addition until sugar is blended. Continue beating until the mixture will stand in very stiff peaks. Fold in nuts and vanilla and blend. Spoon into a lightly greased eight-inch pie pan and make a nest-like shelf, building sides up ½ inch above edge of the pan, but not over the rim. If desired, the meringue can be squeezed through a pastry tube to make a fancy edge. Bake in a slow oven (300 degrees) for 50 to 55 minutes. Cool. Place chocolate and water in a saucepan over low heat. Stir until the chocolate has melted. Cool. Add 1 tablespoon of brandy to chocolate. Whip cream to soft consistency. Fold chocolate mixture into whipped cream. Pile into meringue shell. Chill about 2 hours before serving. (Garnish with shaved chocolate.)

Grenadine of Chicken

(FOR FOUR)

4 chicken breasts	1 tablespoon paprika
¼ cup flour	¼ cup brandy
½ teaspoon salt	1 tablespoon chopped
1 tablespoon olive oil	chives
1 tablespoon butter	1 cup whipping cream

Truffles or mushrooms (optional)

Dip chicken breasts in the flour and salt and shake off as much flour as possible. Sauté in the oil and butter. Add the paprika and brandy. Light and sauté until brandy has cooked away. Add the chives and cream and simmer until reduced by one half.

Serve on rice or green noodles, alone or mixed with croutons, or on Tonnarelli (page 145). Garnish with truffles or mushrooms, if you feel extravagant.

Served with a salad of mixed greens with an oil and vinegar dressing, this makes a pleasant meal — fresh strawberries with warm honey to dip them in for dessert.

This could be called a Potluck if you have a sense of humor. At any rate it is a show-stopper when entertaining guests. We call it

Supreme of Chicken, Nanette

(FOR SIX)

6 chicken breasts	2 cups cream
Salt and pepper	3 egg yolks
¼ teaspoon marjoram	½ cup crabmeat
¼ cup butter	1 tablespoon parsley
½ cup sherry	6 large mushrooms
½ cup grated Swiss cheese	

Remove skin from chicken breasts. Sprinkle with salt and pepper and rub with the marjoram. Sauté in the butter over low heat until done. Remove, and add the sherry to the pan. Cook until almost evaporated. Add the cream and egg yolks. Cook over low heat until thickened. Take enough of the sauce and mix with the crabmeat and parsley to stick the flakes together. Sauté the mushrooms and fill with the crab mixture. Place the breasts in a buttered shallow casserole, place a stuffed mushroom on top of each. Pour the remaining sauce over, add the cheese and run under the broiler until brown. With this you might serve rice with curried fruit.

¼ cup chutney, chopped	½ cup diced pineapple
1 cup melon balls	1 banana, sliced
1 cup Sauterne wine	

Mix and chill. In the meantime —
Mix 1 cup chicken broth with 1 tablespoon curry

18

powder and 1 teaspoon cornstarch. Simmer until thickened. Add a few chopped pistachio nuts or almonds and seedless raisins. Keep warm over hot water. When ready to serve put the cold fruit over hot cooked rice and cover with the sauce — and serve at once.

You hardly need a dessert, but if you do why not buy a pound cake, slice and butter and toast till really brown. Serve with an ice you would pick up at the frozen dessert counter.

Breast of Chicken Prosciutto
(FOR FOUR)

4 chicken breasts
2 tablespoons flour
4 tablespoons butter
4 thin slices prosciutto (Italian ham)
1 white truffle sliced (you may omit)

¼ pound Mozzarella cheese
¾ cup chicken bouillon or water
½ cup dry white wine
2 tablespoons brandy

Remove skin and flatten chicken breasts with a cleaver, or use the heel of your hand. Dust with the flour, and sauté slowly in the butter until brown on both sides. Place the ham on top of each piece, the truffle and a slice of cheese. Add the stock and cook until reduced by one half. Add wine and reduce again. Add brandy and light. Serve with the sauce left in the pan. Use thin slices of any kind of ham if you cannot get prosciutto.

Serve it with saffron rice for instance and under-cooked green beans tossed with lemon butter.

19

Fresh cherries and apricots in a bowl of chipped ice — for a help yourself, all you can eat, dessert.

Chicken Breast in Cream with Apples

(FOR FOUR)

4 broiling-size chicken breasts, or 4 halves of chicken
4 tablespoons butter
2 tablespoons minced onion

4 peeled fresh apple rings, ½ inch thick
¾ cup cider
¼ cup brandy
1 cup heavy cream
Salt and pepper

Sauté the chicken breasts in the butter with the onion over low heat. Poach the apple rings in the cider until soft. Add brandy to the chicken and ignite. Always light brandy and burn off. You destroy the raw taste of the brandy. Add cider left from poaching the apples. Cook at low heat until chicken is tender, about 10 minutes. Add cream and continue cooking until the sauce is thickened. Season to your taste. Place chicken on serving platter, a slice of apple on each piece and pour sauce over all. Run under broiler to brown. I serve this frequently when I wish to impress guests both at N-M and at home. Someone always accuses me of being extravagant enough to serve pheasant. Why disillusion them? Anyhow you may do pheasant or guinea hen this way with success — but I always marinate these birds in a dry white wine for a few hours or overnight.

This is a favorite buffet dinner, because it can be done ahead of time and reheated. I usually serve it with Tonnarelli or brown rice and jumbo asparagus simply dressed with lemon butter. A green salad and for dessert a bowl of fresh strawberries or any other fresh fruit completely covered with either fresh or frozen strawberries put in an electric blender or Foley mill. If I'm ambitious I serve

Chocolate Chip Nut Bars

1 cup cake flour, sifted
½ teaspoon baking powder
¼ teaspoon salt
⅛ teaspoon soda
⅓ cup shortening (butter preferred)

1 cup brown sugar, firmly packed
1 egg slightly beaten
1 teaspoon vanilla
1 package Baker's Semi-Sweet Chocolate Chips

1 cup finely chopped walnut meats

Sift flour once, measure, add baking powder, salt and soda; sift again. Cream shortening, add sugar gradually, and cream together until light and fluffy; add egg and vanilla and mix well after each addition. Then add chocolate chips and nuts; blend. Turn

21

mixture into greased 11 x 7 x 1-inch pan. Bake in moderate oven (350° F.) 25 to 30 minutes. Cut into bars. Remove from pan and cool on cake rack. Cut as large or small as you wish. They are a wonderful cookie with any fruit or ice cream.

You can never have too many chicken recipes. I do not know where I found this, but it is a most favorite Potluck at N-M. Nice for a party too — and you can do it ahead and reheat.

Chicken Crème

(FOR FOUR)

2 1¾-pound broiling
   chickens, whole
½ teaspoon salt
1 teaspoon curry
   powder
¼ cup butter

¼ cup chopped onion
¼ cup water or dry
   white wine
¼ cup brandy
1 cup heavy cream

Rub chickens with salt and curry powder. Put in a casserole with the butter and onion breast side down. Roast at 350° for 30 minutes, baste with the wine or water. Turn breast side up and continue about 45 minutes or until chicken is done (the leg bone will wiggle). Pour the brandy on and light. Remove. Add the cream to juices and cook on top of the stove until a thickened sauce for the chicken. Serve on mixed rices with a dish of chutney on the side. I like to serve little yellow squash steamed, split, and piled high with cooked frozen peas put through a Foley mill, and seasoned with a little nutmeg, butter and salt.

And

Red raspberry ice (store-bought) with hot homemade Scotch Shortbread.

Scotch Shortbread
(TWO CAKES)

1 cup butter
½ cup confectioners' sugar
2 cups flour

¼ teaspoon salt
¼ teaspoon baking powder

Cream butter, add confectioners' sugar and beat until light. Add the flour, salt and baking powder sifted together. Mix well and spoon into cake tins. Pat out to ¼ inch thickness. Prick with a fork. Bake at 350° until a delicate brown — about 20 minutes. Cut in pie shape pieces. Or roll out and cut in squares (24) before baking. Light brown sugar gives it a different flavor and good. Serve it hot. You may reheat many times.

I have a special feeling about Chicken Hash, and I have many recipes. This I use when none of my guests are watching their calories but are pampering their taste buds.

Chicken Hash

(FOR SIX OR EIGHT)

3 tablespoons butter
2 tablespoons flour
2 cups milk
¾ cup light cream
2 tablespoons Parmesan cheese (you may omit)

2 egg yolks beaten
1 quart finely diced
cooked chicken
½ cup cream whipped

Melt the butter in a skillet casserole; add the flour and cook until bubbly. Add milk and cream and cook until thick and creamy. Add the egg yolks and blend thoroughly. Add the chicken. Cover with the whipped cream and cheese and bake at 350° until brown. A wonderful Sunday morning brunch dish, or any other time. I usually have a chafing dish of heavily parslied and chived potato balls to spoon it over, and serve with my favorite breakfast apples.

Baked Apples

(FOR SIX)

6 large Rome Beauty
  apples

4 cups sugar
1 quart water

½ lemon sliced

Peel apple ¼ way down. Remove core. Drop in the sugar and water with the lemon. Bring to a boil, then simmer until apples are tender but not soft. Remove to a casserole, cook syrup down to a jelly (or use currant jelly). Cover top with the jelly. Place in a 350° oven until jelly is completely melted and apples are shiny.

Casserole Chicken and Almonds

(FOR FOUR OR SIX)

3 cups diced raw chicken (frying size or smaller) mixed with one egg white

1 tablespoon olive or salad oil

1 tablespoon butter or margarine

½ cup sliced raw celery — slanty-eyed slices

½ cup sliced bamboo shoots

1 cup sliced Bok Choy

or fresh spinach (you may omit)

¼ cup sliced water chestnuts

½ cup sliced fresh mushrooms

1 tablespoon cornstarch

2 cups chicken consommé

1 tablesoon soy sauce

A handful of snow peas if available

¼ cup blanched almonds

25

Sauté the chicken and egg white that clings to it in the oil and butter until done, about 5 minutes, shaking constantly. Add the vegetables and cover. Cook 3 minutes — the celery should be tender but not soft. Add the cornstarch mixed with the consommé and soy sauce. Add snow peas. Cover and cook 1 minute. Add almonds and serve at once on rice and Chinese noodles (buy them!). If you use dried mushrooms, follow directions on package for using.

One usually does not need a dessert with this dish. It is especially good for the cholesterol watcher (delete the butter for him). However sliced apricots over pineapple ice would be a nice ending for those who need one and even those who do not.

In Texas one hardly thinks of a Potluck supper without a Tamale Pie tucked away somewhere in the recipe file.

Tamale Pie
(FOR SIX OR EIGHT)

12 tamales, cut in 2-inch pieces (canned)
1 quart diced chicken
2 cups chopped corn
2 cups canned tomatoes
½ cup raisins
½ cup sliced, stuffed olives
3 slices bacon, fried crisp and crumbled

1 tablespoon chili powder
¼ cup of butter
½ teaspoon salt
1 teaspoon Lea & Perrins sauce
1 cup chicken consommé
1 cup grated, sharp cheddar cheese

Mix the tamales and chicken with the corn, tomatoes, raisins, olives and bacon. Add the chili powder, salt and Lea & Perrins sauce to the consommé. Place the tamale mix in a buttered 4-quart casserole. Dot with butter. Pour the consommé mixture over. Bake at 300° for 1 hour. Remove. Cover with the cheese and return to oven to brown.

If you are taking the South of the Border seriously, you might serve a guacamole salad with this and some canned or frozen pineapple spears, some toasted pecans and a bit of candy as the ending.

Guacamole

(FOR EIGHT OR TEN)

2 ripe avocados
1 cup peeled, ripe, chopped tomatoes
1 tablespoon finely chopped onion

2 Jalapenos, chopped
1 tablespoon lemon juice or wine vinegar
Salt to taste

Mash avocados, add rest of ingredients. Pile on shredded Iceberg lettuce.

One of the favorite Potlucks at N-M is

Chicken with Eggplant

(FOR FOUR)

2 broilers, split	1 peeled fresh tomato
2 tablespoons butter plus 2 tablespoons olive oil	4 slices green pepper
	8 little white onions
	⅛ teaspoon basil, mixed with
¼ cup sliced mush-rooms, fresh or canned	⅛ teaspoon thyme, and
	½ teaspoon salt
1 small eggplant	1 cup dry white wine

Brown the broilers in the butter and olive oil. Place in a casserole and cover with the mushrooms (sautéed if fresh), the eggplant, peeled and cut into fingers, the tomato cut in quarters, the green pepper and the onions. Sprinkle with the mixed herbs and salt. Add the wine. Cover and cook at 350° for about 45 minutes. A meal in itself — with rice, a few raisins thrown in for good luck — and a green salad.

And

Cherry Torte

2 eggs	canned cherries, drained
1½ cups sugar	
½ cup flour	1 tablespoon butter, melted
1 teaspoon cinnamon	
½ teaspoon soda	¼ teaspoon almond flavoring
¼ teaspoon salt	
3 cups frozen or	½ cup unsalted pecans

Beat eggs, add sugar, beat until thick. Sift flour, cinnamon, soda and salt. Fold into egg mixture. Fold in cherries, butter and flavoring. Grease and flour a shallow 9 x 12-inch tin or casserole. Pour batter in. Scatter nuts on top. Bake at 350° for 1 hour. Cool and serve with whipped cream or cream cheese and this sauce over it. It looks better.

1 tablespoon corn- starch	3 tablespoons sugar 1 tablespoon butter
¼ teaspoon salt	½ teaspoon almond
1 cup cherry juice	flavoring
A few drops of red color	

Mix cornstarch and salt. Mix with one-half the cherry juice. Add to remaining juice which should be boiling. Boil one minute. Remove from fire. Add sugar, butter and flavoring and color. Add more sugar if necessary. Serve at room temperature.

At holiday time one does get tired of leftover turkey and ham. However, ask your neighbors in for Pot-luck supper on Sunday night.

Holiday Turkey and Ham

(FOR FOUR OR SIX)

4 tablespoons butter	¼ cup fine white bread crumbs
3 tablespoons flour	¼ cup Parmesan cheese
2 cups milk	4 or 6 eggs

3 cups diced turkey or
   ham, or some of each
   (and smoked turkey
   is divine)
	1 cup Cheddar-type
	   cheese

	2 tablespoons sherry

29

Melt the butter, add the flour and cook until bubbly. Add milk and cook until thickened. Mix the turkey or ham or both with half of the cream sauce. Place in the buttered casserole. Sprinkle with crumbs and Parmesan cheese and bake at 350° until brown. Remove and break eggs on top. Add the Cheddar cheese to the remaining sauce with the sherry. Cover the eggs and return to the oven until set.

Jumbo asparagus, cooked done, then sprinkled with sliced natural almonds, butter and curry powder, placed in a hot oven until piping hot, is nice with it and peach halves filled with bitter orange marmalade and run under the broiler makes a good combination. One doesn't need dessert.

Chicken and noodles would be the perfect answer for a low-cost supper dish, and no doubt you would have everything in your pantry.

Chicken and Noodles Casserole

4 tablespoons butter
4 tablespoons flour
2 cups chicken con-
   sommé or milk
½ cup light cream
¼ cup dry sherry
1 8-ounce package fine
   noodles
2 8-ounce cans of
   chicken

1 can B in B mush-
   rooms
¼ cup grated Parmesan
   cheese or Swiss
   Gruyère or half and
   half
¼ cup blanched
   almonds
1 teaspoon butter

Make a sauce by melting the butter, add the flour and cook 1 minute. Add consommé or milk, and cream. Cook until thick and smooth, add the sherry. Cook noodles according to directions on package. Drain, wash, and pour into a buttered casserole. Add the chicken, mushrooms, and cream sauce. Sprinkle with the almonds, cheese and butter and bake at 350° until the almonds are brown and the casserole bubbling.

Your favorite tomato aspic recipe with freshly peeled and chopped tomatoes added to it, ½ cup for each cup of liquid, is a nice change and fresh tasting. Lightly flavor store-bought mayonnaise with curry powder and add chopped raw celery and carrots, young onions or whatever you like to serve with it.

For a quick and lazy dessert, lemon ice or sherbet with puréed canned apricots spilled over (put apricots in electric blender), then add sugar and lemon juice to your liking.

When you are feeling blue, your head aches and the world owes you something special, do this soul-soothing

Tiñola
(FOR TWO OR FOUR)

1 3-pound hen	4 pieces celery, or
4 whole raw carrots	leave out
4 whole white onions	1 teaspoon salt
4 whole new potatoes	1 cup cooked peas or
	green beans

Cover the hen with water and the raw vegetables. Simmer slowly until done. Serve in a casserole with peas or beans and chopped parsley added on top. 'Tis good to serve in a soup plate and serve all of it. You could add rice, and leave out the potatoes. I always do this when I am in a crying mood — and I do! And as things look brighter I would make a

Hershey Bar Cake

½ pound butter or	boiler with 2 table-
oleomargarine	spoons of water
2 cups sugar	2½ cups sifted cake
4 eggs	flour
2 teaspoons vanilla	1 cup buttermilk
½ teaspoon salt	¼ teaspoon soda
8 plain Hershey bars	½ cup chopped nuts
melted in a double	

Cream butter and sugar. Add and beat eggs one at a time into the mixture. Add the vanilla and salt and melted Hershey bars. Add the flour and buttermilk mixed with the soda alternately. Fold in the nuts. Bake in a greased angel food pan for 1¾ hours at 325°. Sprinkle with powdered sugar when done, in place of icing. This will keep indefinitely and no icing is necessary.

Crispy Duckling

(FOR FOUR)

Rub a 4- to 5-pound dressed duckling of the Long Island variety with salt and lemon juice. Place ½ an onion with either ½ an orange, apple or turnip in the cavity. Bake at 375° uncovered for 30 minutes. Remove from oven, pour off any grease and return to a 350° oven. Baste with 1 cup Sauterne wine and bake for 1 hour longer, or until done, basting frequently. Remove and refrigerate until cold — or even overnight. Return to oven at 375° and reheat, basting with juices from previous roasting. When ready to serve, strain juices, remove excess fat, and pour over the duck. Add ¼ to ½ cup brandy and light. Serve with the juices only. Grand Marnier poured over and lighted is good too! Serve with Raffetto brand preserved orange slices, hot!

Almost all restaurants serve wild rice with duck. Why not Jerusalem artichokes? You've been dying to try them. Simply scrub, and scrape as you would a carrot. Boil in salted water until tender. Drain, slice and dress with butter, a squeeze of lemon and chopped parsley. And

Brussels Sprouts

1 pound basket or
  2 packages frozen
  brussels sprouts

2 tablespoons chopped
  onion
2 tablespoons butter
1 cup sour cream

Find yourself a Steamette — a kitchen gadget to steam your vegetables in — or put them in a strainer, water in the bottom of a pot and cover, but do not let the vegetables sit in the water. Anyhow, steam the brussels sprouts about 10 minutes, or until tender. Sauté the onion in the butter, add the cream and heat. Add brussels sprouts and mix well.

With duck a light dessert like caramel custard.

Today a hostess in the know can hardly get by without using a crêpe for something or other. They are simple to make and can be used to make an elegant dish out of leftovers.

Basic Crêpe Recipe

1 cup flour   1¾ cups milk
2 eggs   ½ teaspoon salt
      1 tablespoon butter melted

Mix flour and eggs with wire whisk, add rest of ingredients. Brush a 4- or 6-inch skillet with butter, pour in 1 tablespoon batter. Tilt pan to cover bottom. Cook quickly on both sides. Add more milk for a thinner batter. Add 1 tablespoon of sugar for a dessert pancake.

Chicken Crêpe Suzette

(FOR EIGHT)

2 tablespoons butter
1 tablespoon minced
  onion or shallots
2 tablespoons flour
1½ cups half cream,
  half milk

1 cup diced cooked
  chicken
¼ cup sherry
¼ cup grated, Parmesan
  and Swiss Gruyère
¼ cup sliced almonds

Melt butter, add shallots and sauté until yellow. Add flour, cook until bubbly, add cream and milk. Cook until thickened and smooth. Add chicken and sherry to half of the sauce. Place 2 tablespoons in each crêpe, and roll. Place in a buttered shallow casserole. Cover with remaining sauce. Sprinkle with cheese and sliced almonds. Bake at 450° until brown. Substitute crab meat for the chicken or tuna or left over veal.

35

Chicken and Tomato Crêpe

2 cups cooked chicken, cut in strips

1 cup peeled fresh tomato, cut in strips

1 cup heavy cream

1 cup grated Swiss Gruyère cheese

Salt and pepper to taste, and if you like

2 tablespoons canned Jalapenos pepper

Mix together. Roll in crêpes. Place in buttered casserole. Cover with ¼ cup Parmesan cheese plus ½ cup grated Swiss cheese. Bake at 325° until hot and bubbling. Run under broiler 1 minute before serving.

I usually serve hot fruit with a crêpe — for instance, rum-baked pineapple, or a broiled peach half filled with whatever strikes my fancy — and very small crookneck squash, cooked tender, split and covered with buttered peas, sometimes with a few chopped mint leaves or fresh basil added. For dessert a

Jamaican Irish Moss

1 package lemon Jello

½ cup hot water

1 cup orange juice

2 tablespoons sugar

1 tablespoon lemon juice

2 tablespoons grated orange peel

½ cup whipping cream whipped

1 tablespoon dark rum

Add hot water to Jello and melt over hot water. Add orange juice and sugar. When beginning to congeal add lemon juice and grated orange peel. Fold in whipped cream and rum. Pour into mold and let stand a few hours. Serve with orange sections sprinkled with powdered sugar.

Guinea hens are appearing in the markets, sometimes as Christmas gifts, and what to do with them is not a problem. However, as a rule they are dry, so wine, cream and butter do wonderful things to them.

Guinea Hen Madeira

(FOR TWO OR FOUR)

1 2- to 2½-pound
  guinea hen
2 tablespoons butter
Salt and pepper
2 tablespoons grated
  orange peel
1 teaspoon paprika
1 tablespoon currant
  jelly
1 cup chicken con-
  sommé
⅓ cup Madeira
1 cup heavy cream

Rub the hen inside and out with butter, salt and pepper. Roast uncovered at 350° for 30 minutes, basting with more butter and a little water. Add the orange peel, paprika, jelly, consommé and Madeira. Turn. Cover and bake 60 minutes longer, basting frequently. Remove and add the cream. Let simmer for 10 minutes on top of stove, spooning the sauce over frequently.

You never go wrong serving wild rice, and I like to toss a few tiny croutons with it, and grated raw carrots. And sometimes snowpeas and peas — mostly because no one expects it.

37

Belgian endive or Boston lettuce salad tossed with olive oil and lemon juice (4 parts oil to 1 lemon juice and seasoned with freshly ground pepper and salt). For an easy dessert, chocolate ice cream over a few preserved marrons, butterscotch sauce and slivered chocolate. Yummy, high calorie, but who cares once in a while.

Chicken Livers with Apples
(FOR FOUR OR SIX)

1 pound chicken livers
½ cup melted butter
½ cup thinly sliced
  Spanish onion

8 slices peeled and
  cored fresh tart apples
2 tablespoons sugar

Dredge the livers in seasoned flour (flour, salt and paprika) and brown slowly in ¼ cup of melted butter. Sauté in another pan the onions in a little butter and spread over the livers. In the same pan sauté the apple rings which have been sprinkled with the sugar in the remaining butter. Arrange on top of the livers and onions and serve very hot on rice combined with browned almonds, or with fingers of sweet potatoes, Marsala. A nice skillet supper.

I also use this for a buffet dish and add the brown almonds on top, and skip the rice — the men love it. I then go the vegetable route, or very often serve

Vermicelli Salad

1 8-ounce package
  vermicelli
½ cup finely chopped
  celery
2 finely chopped or
  riced hard-cooked
  eggs

1 tablespoon chopped
  green onion
¼ cup chopped parsley
¼ cup of light-bodied
  olive oil
2 tablespoons vinegar
Salt and cracked pepper

¼ cup sour cream

Cook vermicelli and drain dry — do not wash. Add rest of ingredients and toss with two forks. Serve with or without greens.

Fresh mushrooms in sour cream with chicken livers is lovely for Sunday morning brunch, an evening supper after the theater, or just any time if you like chicken livers — and who doesn't?

Mushrooms and Chicken Livers
(FOR FOUR)

1 pound of chicken
  livers
Milk
¼ cup butter
2 tablespoons sherry
  (optional)

2 tablespoons butter
½ pound of fresh mush-
  rooms
1 cup sour cream
2 tablespoons sherry

Very thin toast or sautéed eggplant slices

Cover the livers with milk for an hour. Drain, and sauté in the ¼ cup of butter until brown. Add the

39

sherry (or not) and simmer until completely absorbed. Remove from pan, add 2 tablespoons butter and sauté the mushrooms lightly. Add the sour cream and sherry and heat only until hot. Place the chicken livers on the toast or thin slices of sautéed eggplant and pour the mushrooms over.

I serve fresh pear quarters simmered in butter, a very little brown sugar and lemon juice with this. New flavored rices are on the market — herb, curry, whatever is being dreamed up. These livers are nice with it, as well as other entrées. Look for the rice.

French Toast may be heavenly or awful. I think this recipe extra good. Use it with broiled mushrooms on top — or fresh asparagus — or for creamed entrées.

French Toast

2 eggs   ½ cup cream
⅛ teaspoon salt

Mix and beat thoroughly. Cut bread in ¾ inch triangular pieces. Saturate in mixture. Fry in pure butter until golden brown. Drain on a paper towel. Then put in a 325° oven for a few minutes to obtain a crusty surface. Sprinkle with powdered sugar — or serve with maple syrup or your favorite marmalade or jam.

Seafoods

Casseroles seem to please every member of the family where seafood is concerned.

Cheese and Shrimp Casserole

¼ pound fresh mush-
rooms
2 tablespoons butter
1 pound fresh cooked
shrimp
1½ cups cooked rice
1½ cups grated aged
Cheddar cheese

½ cup cream
3 tablespoons catsup
½ teaspoon Worcester-
shire sauce
½ teaspoon salt
Dash of pepper

Slice mushrooms, sauté slowly in butter 10 minutes or until tender. Mix lightly with shrimp, rice and cheese. Combine cream, catsup, Worcestershire sauce and seasonings; add to shrimp mixture. Pour into casserole, chill overnight, if desired. Bake in moderate oven (350°) 25 minutes. A hearty flavor. Serve with broccoli dressed with butter, grated lemon peel and chopped pimiento, and perhaps this —

43

Piquante Salad Bowl

1 peeled, quartered tomato
1 cup cooked green beans

1 head lettuce, broken
¼ cup chopped parsley
2 hard cooked eggs, chopped or riced

Toss and serve with this warm salad dressing —

1 cup whipping cream
4 tablespoons olive oil
2 tablespoons prepared mustard

2 tablespoons white vinegar
1 tablespoon dried tarragon

Cook over hot water until thick. Serve warm over salad greens.

For dessert a combination of whatever ices or sherbets you can pick up at the corner drive-in. It is just as easy to carry 3 pints or more home as 1 — and whoever is the recipient thinks you gave the dessert some thought, whether you did or not. Spill a little Cointreau over for good measure.

Crabmeat and Almonds

(FOR FOUR OR SIX)

¼ cup butter
1 cup blanched
  almonds
2 pounds lump crab-
  meat

2 cups whipping cream
1 teaspoon arrowroot
¼ cup finely chopped
  parsley
Salt and pepper

Slices of heavily buttered, oven-made toast, or
large croutons, or patty shells (buy) spread
with Smithfield ham.

Melt the butter and sauté almonds until slightly
brown. Add crabmeat and brown delicately. Shake
the skillet or pot instead of stirring, to keep the
pieces intact. Add the cream and arrowroot and cook
2 minutes. Add parsley and season to your taste.
Spoon over the toast.

Or omit the almonds and flavor with sherry. Serve
either combination over broiled pineapple, mushrooms or cold avocado slices. I serve this frequently
for bridal luncheons. It is light and distinctive
enough in flavor to make even a nervous bride inter-
ested. With it a salad of fresh fruits cut in definable
pieces (one does like to know whether it is canta-
loupe or peaches he is eating). Poppy-seed dressing,
of course! For a vegetable, I suggest freshly cooked
green beans tossed with lots of parsley in the butter.
Parsley when used with a heavy hand makes a green
vegetable taste more green, a little grated lemon
peel, too!

Poppy-Seed Dressing

(From HELEN CORBITT'S COOKBOOK)

1½ cups sugar
2 teaspoons dry mustard
2 teaspoons salt
⅔ cup vinegar

3 tablespoons onion juice
2 cups salad oil — but never olive oil (I use Wesson)

3 tablespoons poppy-seeds

Mix sugar, mustard, salt, and vinegar. Add onion juice and stir it in thoroughly. Add oil slowly, beating constantly, and continue to beat until thick. Add poppyseeds and beat for a few minutes. Store in a cool place or the refrigerator, but not near the freezing coil.

It is easier and better to make with an electric mixer or blender, using medium speed, but if your endurance is good you may make it by hand with a rotary beater. The onion juice is obtained by grating a large white onion on the fine side of a grater, or putting in an electric blender, then straining. (Prepare to weep in either case.) If the dressing separates, pour off the clear part and start all over, adding the poppy-seed mixture slowly, but it will not separate unless it becomes too cold or too hot.

A delightful luncheon or dinner casserole using crabmeat is this one.

Crabmeat Chantilly

(FOR FOUR OR SIX)

1 pound lump crab- meat	2 cups light cream Salt and pepper
2 tablespoons butter	2 packages asparagus
½ cup sherry	(frozen)
2 tablespoons flour	1 cup whipped cream

4 tablespoons Parmesan cheese

Sauté the crabmeat lightly in the butter. Add the
sherry and simmer until reduced by one half. Add
the flour and cream, season and cook until thickened,
fork-stir to keep the crabmeat in lumps (or you
might use canned cream of mushroom or celery
soup), and heat. Cook the asparagus and drain.
Place in the bottom of a well-buttered casserole.
Pour the crabmeat over, spread the whipped cream
over, sprinkle with the cheese and brown under a
low flame.

Substitute any seafood, or even chicken, for the
crabmeat, add any vegetable in place of the asparagus.
Add slices of avocado before spreading the whipped
cream — or mushrooms — or browned almonds. It
is a versatile dish, high in calories, but worth it. Nice
for a buffet supper. A pretty dish when served in a
colored enamel skillet casserole — Kobenstyle for instance. Serve with thin rye bread buttered with
sweet butter, thick slices of tomatoes sprinkled with
a clear French dressing and dill. A lemon chiffon
cake made from a mix with a real lemony butter
cream icing.

47

I like to combine the flavor and texture of seafood with other flavors. For instance:

King Crab and Chipped Beef Casserole

1 pound frozen King Crab Legs or canned crabmeat
butter
1 cup sliced mushrooms, canned or fresh
2 tablespoons sherry
2 tablespoons flour
2 cups milk or half milk, half cream
1 4-ounce jar chipped beef
¼ cup olives
½ cup white bread crumbs
2 tablespoons melted butter

Cut crabmeat into chunks as large as possible. Sauté in butter, remove and add mushrooms, and sauté 1 minute. Add sherry and continue cooking until reduced by one half. Add flour and cook until bubbly. Add milk and cook until thickened. Add crabmeat, chipped beef, and olives. Simmer until hot. Correct seasoning if necessary, but taste before adding. Pour into a buttered shallow casserole and sprinkle with crumbs mixed with the melted butter. Bake at 350° until hot and bubbly and crumbs are brown, or spoon over baking-powder biscuits.

Exotic Rice

(FOR SIX OR EIGHT)

1¼ cups rice
¼ cup butter
2½ cups chicken
    bouillon

½ cup toasted almonds
¼ cup golden or white
    raisins
Salt and pepper

Brown rice in butter, add chicken bouillon, cover and cook in a 350° oven for 40 minutes. Add rest of ingredients and press into a buttered ring mold. Bake at same temperature for 10 minutes. Unmold carefully and fill center with buttered fresh green beans finely cut (slanty-eyed). I think this rice is wonderful with everything. With it I might serve for dessert —

Raspberry Frango

1 cup sugar
4 egg yolks
1 cup hot milk

Beat egg yolks, add sugar and hot milk. Cook until thickened. Cool. Add:

1 cup mashed raspberries, fresh or frozen
    (put in a blender)
1 tablespoon lemon juice
2 cups cream whipped

Freeze in freezing compartment or in individual services in your deep freeze. It is a wonderful ending to any meal. Pretty decorated with whole berries.

49

Lump crabmeat is a delicacy you should cultivate. Expensive but worth it, but really not too much so, as a little will go quite a way toward making an interesting meal.

The delicate flavor and texture of lump crabmeat has an affinity with both fruits and vegetables, and especially so with white meat of chicken and the flavor of smoked meats.

A Crabmeat Casserole

(FOR EIGHT OR TEN)

4 tablespoons butter
4 tablespoons flour
1¼ cups milk
1 teaspoon salt
A couple of twists from a black-pepper mill
1 tablespoon Madeira (you may omit)
1 tablespoon lemon juice

4 egg yolks
1 can fresh crabmeat
1 cup finely slivered ham
1 cup finely slivered white meat of chicken
4 egg whites — (one extra will not do it any harm)

Parmesan cheese

Melt the butter, add the flour and cook until bubbly. Add the milk and cook until thick. Add seasonings and Madeira and lemon juice. Add egg yolks and crabmeat, ham and chicken. Beat egg whites until stiff. Fold in cooled crab mixture and pour into an unbuttered 3-quart casserole. Sprinkle with Parmesan cheese and bake at 350° for 45 minutes (in a warm water bath). Serve with Newburg sauce or a thin cream sauce with slivers of pineapple added to it.

With it, canned or fresh pineapple fingers sprinkled with brown sugar and fresh mint or flakes and baked at the same time. A tray of thick slices of avocado and tomato quarters, and hot bread sticks would make an interesting supper, with a tray of homemade cookies like these.

Bourbon Cookies

2 cups brown sugar
1 cup butter
4 cups flour
4 eggs
1 teaspoon nutmeg
1 teaspoon cloves
1 cup bourbon

3 teaspoons soda — dissolved in
2 tablespoons buttermilk
¼ pound citron or candied fruit
2 pounds pecans

1½ pounds raisins

Mix in order given and drop by half teaspoonfuls on buttered cookie sheet. Bake at 350° F.

Keep this recipe in mind for Christmas — and

Angel Cookies

¼ pound butter   ¾ cup sugar

Cream together — Add:

1 8-ounce package dates, chopped

Boil together for 3 minutes — Add:

1 cup nut meats   1 teaspoon vanilla
1 cup Rice Krispies

Cool and roll in Angel Flake Coconut. Nice for holiday giving.

Economical entrées can sometimes appeal to our taste buds more than lobster and champagne. These I remember and still serve with pleasure.

Salmon Soufflé

(FOR FOUR OR SIX)

3 tablespoons butter   Pinch of thyme
3 tablespoons flour   (you may omit)
½ teaspoon curry   Salt and pepper
   powder   1 cup milk
1½ cups fresh or   4 eggs, separated
   canned salmon
   flakes

Melt the butter, add the flour and seasonings and cook until bubbly. Add the milk, bring to a boil and boil for 1 minute, but start counting when it boils, stirring constantly. Remove from stove. Add egg yolks beaten until light and the salmon flaked and free from bones and skin. Cool. Fold in the egg whites stiffly beaten. Pour into a buttered casserole and bake at 375° for 45 minutes in a hot water bath. (Use the same recipe for left-over chicken or ham or any cooked fish.) Serve with

BENGAL SAUCE

1 tablespoon butter	Salt
1 tablespoon flour	½ teaspoon curry
1 cup half milk, half	powder
cream (or whole	2 teaspoons grated
milk)	coconut
¼ cup slivered blanched almonds	

Melt butter, add flour, cook a few seconds. Add milk and cream mixture and cook until smooth and thickened. Add seasonings, coconut and nuts. A good sauce for any soufflé or for croquettes. Serve with canned peaches filled with chutney and baked until hot, or curried pears. Any green vegetable goes well with salmon, but because my mother served peas with salmon I usually do, combined with cooked, fresh white onions or scallions, or the canned Belgian carrots, heavily parslied. A cabbage and celery coleslaw lightly dressed, so it is really crunchy. For dessert, preserved ginger spilled over a loaf of cream cheese sprinkled with grated lemon peel and toasted unsalted crackers.

I find this a wonderful buffet idea and usually serve it on a cocktail buffet with small silver-dollar-size patty shells (buy them).

Shrimp, Almonds and Chives

(FOR SIX OR EIGHT)

2 pounds PDQ shrimp (peeled, deveined and quick-frozen)
4 tablespoons butter
¼ cup brandy

1 quart heavy cream
½ teaspoon paprika
Salt and pepper to taste
1 cup browned whole almonds
¼ cup chopped chives

Defrost the shrimp — or buy raw shrimp in the market and peel. Sauté in the butter until they begin to turn pink. Add the brandy and light. When it burns off, add the cream and cook until thick. Season. Add the almonds and chives. Keep hot over hot water.

A bowl of salad greens with slivers of Swiss cheese and ham and a tart French dressing, herb-buttered bread and partially frozen peaches with lemon ice would make a good combination of flavors.

There comes a time when you cannot find the fresh fish you would like to have. This recipe is especially good for frozen fish of a white variety, but you may use any fish.

Fish Fillets Thermidor

(FOR FOUR)

1 pound package fish
   fillets
Dry white wine
4 tablespoons butter
4 tablespoons flour
1 teaspoon salt

1 cup milk
1 cup cream
¼ cup sherry
1 can B in B mush-
   rooms
½ cup Parmesan cheese

Poach the fish in ½ water, ½ wine. Remove, drain, and place in a buttered casserole. Melt the butter, add the flour and salt. Cook until bubbly. Add the milk, cream and sherry, and cook until thick. Cover the fish with the mushrooms, then the sauce. Sprinkle with the cheese and bake in a 350° oven until brown and sizzling.

Serve new potatoes swished around in a little sugar and butter that has melted until brown before adding the potatoes, and a salad of raw spinach and tomatoes with a Basic French Dressing.

Basic French Dressing

⅓ cup olive oil
2 tablespoons vinegar,
   or lemon juice, or a
   mixture of both

½ teaspoon salt
Freshly ground pepper
¼ teaspoon dry
   mustard

Orégano, tarragon or rosemary

Dribble oil over broken salad greens in a zigzag formation. Repeat with rest of ingredients. Toss lightly and let your salad breathe. For a Caesar Dressing add a coddled egg (1 minute) before tossing, and anchovies. If you are garlic minded, add the garlic to the oil several hours beforehand.

And — Lemon Jelly. Who couldn't whip this up in a hurry?

Lemon Jelly Whip
(FOR SIX OR EIGHT)

2 lemons   2 tablespoons sugar
              2 packages Lemon Jello

Dissolve Jello according to package directions. When just about congealed, whip and add the sugar dissolved in the juice and grated rind of the 2 lemons. Serve with or without whipped cream.

Another easy fish dish.

Red Snapper with Coconut

Dip fillets of red snapper in pineapple juice. Dot generously with butter, sprinkle with salt and paprika. Bake at 300° until partially done. Cover with fresh grated coconut, or Angel Flake. Return to oven until done. Baste frequently. Serve with fresh lime slices.

56

I like cucumbers with fish, even hot ones. Just peel and slice, and steam until tender, 1 minute. Drain, season with salt and pepper and add enough sour cream to "stick 'em." Run under broiler to brown. New potatoes partially peeled, boiled and rolled in chopped parsley and chives, and I mean rolled not just sprinkled, and who doubts that lemon pie goes with fish?

Lemon Pie

4 tablespoons corn-starch	½ teaspoon salt
4 tablespoons flour	1½ cups sugar
	1½ cups boiling water

Combine and cook until thick. Cook over hot water for 20 minutes. Remove and add 2 tablespoons butter and 5 egg yolks. Continue to cook over hot water until thick. Cool and add ⅓ cup lemon juice and 1 tablespoon grated lemon peel. Pour into a baked 9-inch pie shell. Beat the egg whites to soft peak stage, then beat in ½ cup sugar gradually. Add 1 teaspoon lemon juice. Pile on pie, roughly and high. (For Sky-Hi — add 2 more egg whites and 2 tablespoons sugar.) Bake about 5 minutes at 425° — but watch it — or cover with whipped cream in place of the meringue.

Beef

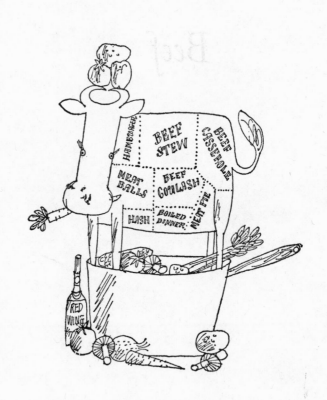

Why fight it? There is nothing greater than a good stew. I know! There are never any leftovers. By the same rule, there is nothing worse than a poor one.

This stew usually finds its way onto my Potluck menu. For 4 or 400 it never fails for contentment.

Beef Stew

(FOR SIX)

2½ pounds lean beef stew meat, cut in 1-inch cubes
1 tablespoon flour
½ cup finely chopped onion
½ bud garlic (you may omit)
1½ quarts canned consommé or water
½ cup Burgundy or sherry (you may omit, but the stew tastes better with it)
1 tablespoon sugar
Salt and pepper

Dust the meat with flour and sauté with the onions and garlic until well browned, and the onions are soft. Add the sugar, cook one minute, add consommé and wine and cook at low heat until done, about 2½ hours. Season with salt and pepper. If you like a thicker gravy, slightly thicken with flour or arrowroot. The delight of a stew, however, is a thin sauce.

Serve on rice or noodles, and if you like vegetables with it, add them, freshly cooked, after the stew is completely done. Leftover vegetables have no place in a stew.

Vary the stew by adding sautéed chicken livers and mushrooms, or slivers of cooked ham, or cover

61

with a thin pie crust, sprinkle with Parmesan cheese (a goodly amount) and bake at 350° until done, about 20 minutes. In the Zodiac Room, we serve this stew on a layer of crisp, crisp hashed brown potatoes. A crisp salad of Bibb lettuce and fresh peeled tomatoes, or a crisp coleslaw will never argue with a stew. An ice cream pie for dessert, and I like this one. Coffee ice cream in a coconut crust with butterscotch sauce and whipped cream, with just a dash of instant coffee added to it.

COCONUT CRUST

2 tablespoons butter
1 tablespoon milk
⅔ cup sifted confectioners' sugar
1½ cups Angel Flake Coconut

Heat butter and milk, until butter is melted. Add sugar and coconut. Mix and spread over bottom and sides of 9-inch pie pan. Bake at 350° for 5 minutes. Remove and chill until firm. Fill with ice cream. Use a wooden spoon and have the ice cream as firm as possible. *Do not melt ice cream then pour in.* Cover with foil or wax paper and deep freeze. Keep on hand for a quick dessert for any time.

This is good any time of the year.

Oven Stew

(FOR FOUR OR SIX)

2½ tablespoons butter
¼ cup celery, minced
¼ cup green peppers, thinly sliced
1 clove garlic, minced (you may omit)
½ cup onions, sliced
2 pounds beef stew meat or round steak
2½ tablespoons flour

¼ teaspoon pepper
½ teaspoon sugar
1 fresh tomato peeled and diced
1 4-ounce can mushrooms
2 cups broth or water
½ cup dry red wine
½ cup pimento-stuffed, sliced olives

1½ teaspoons salt

Melt the butter in a skillet. Add the celery, green peppers, garlic and onions. Sauté until softened and slightly browned. Cut the meat into 1-inch cubes. Dust with the flour and seasonings. Add to the skillet; sauté until browned. Stir in the sugar, tomato, canned mushrooms and liquid, and wine. Transfer to a buttered 3-quart casserole; cover. Let stand several hours. Bake 2 hours in a moderate oven, 350°. Stir in the sliced olives 5 minutes before completion.

Serve with cognac baby carrots and wheat pilaff (you buy this at your good grocery shops).

63

Carrots in Cognac

(FOR FOUR)

2 cups slivered raw   1 teaspoon sugar
   carrots   1 cup butter
           ⅓ cup cognac

Place in covered baking dish and bake at 350° until
tender, about ½ hour.

Beef Patties, Madeira

(FOR FOUR)

2 pounds ground lean   4 slices toast, cut to fit
   beef   the patties
½ cup Madeira   1 small can liver paté
Salt and pepper   4 mushroom caps,
⅛ pound (½ stick)   browned in butter
   butter

Mix beef with 1 tablespoon of butter and 1 teaspoon
salt. Form into 4 patties. Marinate the patties in
the Madeira for at least 1 hour. Remove. Sprinkle
with cracked pepper and sauté in the butter over high
heat for 3 minutes on either side. Place toast in the
remaining butter and sauté. Place a pattie on each
slice and cover with a slice of the liver paté. Top
each with a mushroom cap. Pour the remaining
marinade from the steaks into the pan and simmer for
3 minutes. Pour over steaks and place in a 400° oven
for 3 minutes. Do tenderloin steaks the same way.

When ground beef is definitely in the budget picture, mix the beef with butter and salt, form into patties, and sauté in the butter. Then add ¼ cup of Burgundy wine and simmer until wine is gone. Serve with a small ball of butter mixed with Roquefort cheese or prepared mustard on top of each pattie.

Beef patties for outdoor cooking are better I think if you add ¼ cup of cracked ice to each pound of meat, when you mix.

I always say mashed potatoes taste even better if put into a casserole, spread with whipped cream and shredded cheese — then baked until brown on top. And they go especially well with hamburgers or meat loaves. Relishes, hearty ones like carrot sticks, celery hearts, cherry tomatoes, olives, help you forget a salad. For dessert why anything at all — but à la mode it.

For those who refuse to take cooking seriously, but still want to make an impression, we have the answer.

Fondue Bourguignonne

(FOR FOUR OR SIX)

2 pounds tender filet of beef, cut in ¾- to 1-inch cubes or thin slices

1½ cups good grade olive oil or

1 cup oil and ½ cup of melted butter

A metal fondue pot or chafing dish or electric skillet — but to be proper and impressive — the pot, please

Long-tined fondue forks with heat-proof handles

Place uncooked beef on a wooden tray or board; either place on table or pass for guests to help themselves. The oil should be boiling, then kept hot with Sterno during the cooking process and placed on the table. Each guest spears a piece of meat, then cooks it himself in the hot oil. You should also have a variety of sauces or condiments for them to dip the meat into. For instance, Lawry's Seasoned Salt and Pepper, or one I make myself, 4 tablespoons of salt, 1 tablespoon cracked pepper, ½ teaspoon paprika, ½ teaspoon curry powder, pinch of nutmeg and orégano. Or any preserved spiced fruit juice mixed with enough dry mustard to make a paste (this is good with any kind of meat); or 1 cup mayonnaise mixed with ¼ cup chopped capers and ¼ cup chopped parsley; or ¼ pound of butter mixed with 2 tablespoons of anchovy paste. You can really let your imagination run riot for the sauces to dip the meat in.

I have pieces of fresh parsley to fry also, and slices of sweet onion. Your guests are so busy you only need to provide a bowl of relishes, quite hardy ones, hot French bread and coffee.

Hearty casserole dishes are good for parties where you know appetites are keen, like after a football game, merry elbow-lifting, skiing or whatever. This you may do ahead of time, and bake while socializing — or complete and reheat.

Beef Roulade

(FOR FOUR OR EIGHT)

8 thin slices beef, about 4 inches square (round or bottom butt)
Salt and pepper
2 dill pickles
1 cup thinly sliced onion
2 tablespoons butter

4 slices bacon
2 cups leftover brown gravy or slightly thickened beef consommé. I have seen brown gravy in cans on the grocer's shelf. What next?

¼ cup red Burgundy, or not

Lay beef flat on a meat board, flatten with a cleaver or edge of a china plate. Sprinkle with salt and pepper. Quarter the pickles lengthwise. Sauté the onions in the butter until yellow, but do not brown. Cut bacon in half. Place in center of the beef ¼ pickle, ½ slice bacon and ⅛th of the sautéed onion

(1 tablespoon). Roll and secure with a toothpick. Brown in a skillet in hot cooking oil or fat. Place in a shallow casserole. Cover with the brown gravy and wine. Cover and bake at 350° for 1 hour. Uncover and bake 1 hour longer, or until tender. Serve with noodles or the Pasta Ricotta. Teen-age boys and girls like this! Serve 1 or 2 depending on how generous you are.

A salad of cooked vegetables serves two purposes

(FOR FOUR OR EIGHT)

1 cup cooked, diced carrots	1 cup diced celery
	¼ cup capers
1 cup cooked, diced green beans	¼ cup sliced olives
	2 whole tomatoes, peeled and diced
1 cup cooked peas	

Mix and combine with just enough mayonnaise to hold together. Decorate with riced hard-cooked egg — or leave out the tomatoes and stuff whole tomatoes with the vegetables. Serve with fresh salad greens. For dessert, cold Delicious apples and raisins.

One could pick up the ingredients for this skillet dish on the way home from a busy day in town. It takes about one hour to prepare, and with a green salad would please even a steak-and-potato-and-green-bean man.

Oriental Steak

(F O R   F O U R)

1 pound beef chuck or round, cut in thin strips

¼ cup olive or salad oil

1 clove garlic, minced

1 teaspoon soy sauce

½ teaspoon salt

¼ cup water

1 cup green pepper, cut in strips (2 medium size)

½ cup slivered celery

1 cup thinly sliced onion

1 cup consommé (I prefer chicken)

1 tablespoon cornstarch

½ teaspoon sugar

2 fresh tomatoes, peeled and cut in eighths

Brown beef in the oil. Add garlic and cook until garlic is yellow. Add soy sauce, salt, water. Cook about ½ hour. Add vegetables (except tomatoes), consommé, cover and cook 5 minutes at fast heat. Stir in the cornstarch and sugar blended with a little water. Add tomatoes and cook until they are hot.

Serve over rice. Snow peas boiled 1 minute in a small amount of water, dressed with very little butter are good — or any vegetable. Sliced kumquats over vanilla ice cream for dessert.

Potluck may take on an elegant touch, and as my friends say, "I dearly love your kind of Potluck."

Beef Tenderloin in Claret

1 3-pound piece of beef
   tenderloin, trimmed
   for roasting
Salt and pepper
4 young onions or
   shallots
          Brandy

4 tablespoons butter
½ cup claret
½ cup beef consommé
1 teaspoon cornstarch
   or arrowroot
½ teaspoon lemon juice

Roast the tenderloin, rubbed with salt and pepper, at 300° for 1 hour. Sauté the onions in the butter, add the claret and cook until reduced by half. Add the consommé mixed with the cornstarch and simmer until thickened. Add the lemon juice and pour over the filet. Run under broiler until the whole thing is bubbling; add 2 tablespoons of brandy at the table and light.

Serve with halves of tomatoes covered with sour cream and baked, asparagus, and mushrooms (fresh or canned) stuffed with chopped, cooked chicken livers. An elegant dish when you feel like celebrating. It calls for an elegant dessert too . . . such as

Mousse au Chocolat

¾ cup butter
1½ cups sugar
½ teaspoon almond extract
1 tablespoon brandy
3 eggs, separated

½ pound semi-sweet chocolate or chocolate chips
¼ cup slivered toasted almonds or marrons
2 cups whipped cream

Stir butter until creamy. Blend in sugar, almond extract, brandy and egg yolks. Melt the chocolate and add with the almonds to the butter mixture. Fold in egg whites beaten stiff. Fold in whipped cream. Pour into a mold, or one lined with lady fingers. Refrigerate several hours. Unmold and decorate with whipped cream and layers of shaved semi-sweet chocolate. You do this by leaving the chocolate at room temperature for a few hours, then scraping the surface with a heavy sharp knife (or silver one) toward you. Be not stingy! Or you could use toasted natural almonds, but the chocolate is more spectacular. Add a bit of instant coffee to whipped cream to take away what I call the dead taste. Freeze, too, if you wish before decorating — a nice do-ahead dessert — and the men, they love it.

Low-calorie main dishes are much in conversational vogue today. Why not face the issue, and do use as many natural foods as possible, without butter, without flour and fixin's. This I use and like.

Beef Burgundy in Casserole

(FOR FOUR)

2 or 3 pound piece of lean beef chuck, blade, or sirloin butt
1 tomato, diced
2 fresh carrots, scraped and quartered
2 medium onions, peeled
2 mushrooms, peeled

2 stalks celery, cut in fourths
1 clove garlic (optional)
1 cup canned consommé
½ cup burgundy
Salt and pepper as needed

Chopped parsley or any green vegetable

Brown meat quickly in a skillet. Remove to a casserole. Add vegetables, consommé, wine and seasonings. Cover and bake at 350° for about 2 hours or less. Serve with chopped parsley or a green vegetable sprinkled over the top. The delicate flavor of the juices and wine are cooked into the vegetables, so be sure to eat all of them. Do thick hamburger patties the same way.

I am becoming fond of pastas made from artichoke flour. Less calories! Cook in boiling salted water until tender, drain, do not wash — and toss with dry cottage cheese and cracked pepper until well blended. Low calorie and tasty. Toss in a few poppy seeds for added flavor.

Spicy Brisket of Beef

(FOR FOUR OR SIX)

3 pounds fresh beef brisket
1 teaspoon salt
¼ teaspoon pepper
1 sliced onion
1 whole piece celery
½ cup chili sauce
1 can beer
¼ cup chopped parsley

Place beef in casserole. Season and cover with the onion, celery and chili sauce. Add ¼ cup water, and roast uncovered in a 325° oven until brown. Pour beer over, cover and bake at the same temperature for about 3 hours, or until tender. Remove meat and strain off all the fat. Add chopped parsley. Cut in thin slices and serve with the juices. This is no dish for a weakling, so serve hashed brown potatoes and sugar buttered carrots and onions with it.

You might like to have a relish with this also. The same old thing in a new dress is:

Cranberry Horseradish Mousse

2 cups whole cran-
   berry sauce
1 cup sour cream
3 tablespoons horse-
   radish sauce
1 tablespoon lemon
   juice
¼ cup grated raw carrot
1 tablespoon gelatin
¼ cup cold water

Combine first five ingredients. Add gelatin to water. Heat over hot water until melted. Add to cranberry mixture. Pour into mold and chill.

When small fry bring home unexpected guests, give them a

"Sloppy Joe" Hamburger

1½ pounds ground beef
½ cup chopped onion
1 cup chopped celery
2 tablespoons butter
   or salad oil
2 tablespoons brown
   sugar
1½ teaspoons salt
½ bottle chili sauce
2 tablespoons vinegar
¼ cup chopped green
   pepper
Hamburger buns

Brown beef, onions and celery in oil. Add rest of ingredients and simmer until thick and well blended. Spoon over hot toasted buns. Go ahead and freeze

74

the beef mixture for a quickie for the whole family. A slice of American Cheddar cheese on top of the bun will never be amiss.

Give the children ice cream cones. They always love them or snowmen if you are ambitious. Snowmen are made by putting two balls of vanilla ice cream — one smaller than the other — one on top of the other, anchored to the plate with either a white cake circle or meringue shell. Use raisins for the features and the buttons on his coat. A whipped cream cap, a maraschino tassel and candy sticks for arms.

Another "sloppy" deal is called a

Yankee Sandwich

1 pound sliced frank-
furters
2 cups canned baked
beans

¼ cup chopped onion
⅓ cup chili sauce

Mix, bring to a boil, simmer for 5 minutes — serve on toasted buns.

Leftover beef, veal or lamb, or for that matter fish or fowl too, goes into what we call

Malayan Skillet

(FOR EIGHT OR TEN)

3 tablespoons butter
1 tablespoon curry powder
¼ green pepper cut in strips
½ medium onion sliced thin
4 mushrooms sliced
4 cups leftover meat cut in strips
½ cup Pineapple Chunks
2 bananas

1 cup medium cream sauce, or leftover gravy, or canned mushroom soup
1 cup light cream
¼ cup toasted whole almonds
1 canned pimiento cut in strips
Salt and pepper

Melt the butter in a large serving skillet. Add the curry and cook 1 minute. Add green pepper, onion, and mushrooms. Sauté at medium heat until onion is yellow but not brown. Add the meat; sauté until thoroughly heated. Add fruit and cream sauce or gravy. Heat and fork-stir to keep from mashing the bananas. Add cream, almonds, and pimiento. Cook until thoroughly blended. Taste for any added salt and pepper. Serve on hot rice. This is especially good for meat that has been cooked and frozen. The flavors of the ingredients destroy any "left over" taste.

German Coleslaw

Cover one head of cabbage, shredded fine, with boiling water for five minutes. Drain dry and add:

2 tablespoons finely chopped onion, or leave it out
¼ cup vinegar
½ teaspoon salt
¼ teaspoon pepper
3 tablespoons chopped parsley
3 tablespoons olive oil

Toss together, and add a cup of sour cream.

Another good way to use leftover beef is with mustard. Spread both sides of the thinly sliced leftover meat with prepared mustard and coat with fresh bread crumbs. Sprinkle the slices with melted butter and sauté in more butter until golden brown. Garnish with chopped egg and chopped parsley or not.

Shortribs

4 pounds shortribs from choice beef, cut in 3-inch pieces
1 cup tomatoes
1 cup water or con-sommé
½ cup burgundy
¼ cup finely chopped onion

2 tablespoons prepared horseradish
1 teaspoon salt
¼ teaspoon pepper
¼ teaspoon ground ginger
2 bay leaves

Brown the shortribs in a skillet and drain off the fat that cooks out of them. Mash the tomatoes to a pulp and add with the rest of the ingredients. Cover and bake at 350° until done, about 2½ to 3 hours. Remove to a hot platter, strain the sauce and pour over. Thicken slightly, if you like, with arrowroot dissolved in a little cold water.

I like to add halves of fresh cherry tomatoes or peeled tomato quarters to the sauce and just heat enough to make them hot, and sprinkle chopped chives or parsley over the top. New potatoes cooked in their jackets, sprinkled with Parmesan cheese, and any green vegetable go well with shortribs, and boiled fresh white onions simmered in butter with a few raisins give an interesting flavor to the meal — also conversation. A really surprise dessert with them —

Chantilly Torte

6 egg yolks
1½ cups sugar
2½ tablespoons flour
1 teaspoon baking
powder

3 cups ground pecans
6 egg whites, beaten
stiff
3 cups cream,
whipped

Beat egg yolks, add sugar and beat for 15 minutes.
Sift flour and baking powder and add gradually to
the sugar and eggs. Add ground pecans and fold in
the egg whites. Bake in buttered cake pans at 350°
for 30 minutes. Fill and cover with whipped cream
and layers of shaved semi-sweet chocolate.

Or bake in sheets, pile high with the whipped
cream and shaved chocolate for Black Forest Cake.

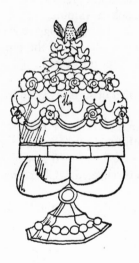

Beef and Eggplant Casserole

1 medium-size egg-
plant
1 pound ground beef
2 tablespoons finely
chopped onion
¼ cup finely chopped
green pepper (drop
in boiling water 1
minute before chop-
ping)

2 tablespoons olive
oil
1 tablespoon flour
¾ teaspoon salt
¼ teaspoon orégano
1 cup chopped,
canned or fresh
peeled tomato
1¼ cups grated sharp
Cheddar cheese

Peel and slice eggplant. Cook in boiling water until
tender but not soft. Drain. Brown the beef in the
oil with the onion and green pepper. Add flour and
seasonings. Cook 2 minutes. Add tomatoes and
cook until thick. Arrange in layers with the eggplant
and cheese leaving cheese for the top layer. Bake at
350° for 30 minutes uncovered.

This needs a salad of sorts, as I call it (for six).

1 bunch watercress
6 scallions with tops,
sliced
1 stalk of celery, slivered

1 celery cabbage sliced
in 1-inch slices
6 ripe olives, sliced
Clear French dressing

Toss together, let stand 30 minutes in ice box before
serving.

In your deep freeze at all times keep this nut cake. You could bring it out for dessert for this casserole meal — you could use it for tea parties. The recipe came from Catherine Cutrer, the wife of a Houston Mayor, through Margaret Hull my favorite recipe gossiper.

Nut Cake

1 pound butter
2 cups sugar, sifted
6 eggs, separated
3 cups cake flour
¾ pound candied cherries
¼ pound candied pineapple
5 cups nuts, broken
2 ounces lemon extract

Cream butter and sugar. Add beaten yolks, flour, finely chopped fruit, nuts and lemon extract. Beat egg whites until stiff but not dry, and fold into batter. Bake 1 hour at 300°. Can be baked in 4 small loaf pans or one large pan.

A good meat sauce is one thing you can keep in your icebox or deep freeze, and this one I like because it is gentle with my taste buds.

Meat Sauce

¼ pound salt pork diced
½ cup minced onion
1 cup minced celery
½ cup minced carrots
1 tablespoon butter
2 pounds ground beef
¼ cup white wine
1½ cups chopped fresh peeled tomatoes
2 cups light cream

Sauté the salt pork until brown. Add the onion, celery, carrots and cook until they are transparent. Add the butter, meat, wine and tomatoes. Simmer for 1½ hours. Add cream and continue cooking until thick.

This is wonderful with Lasagna (a wide noodle) using a mixture of Parmesan and Swiss Gruyère cheese with it. You cook the noodles. Make a thin cream sauce made with coffee cream instead of milk, with a pinch of nutmeg added. Place a layer of cream sauce in bottom of casserole, then noodles, then meat sauce, then cheese, repeat for 2 layers of each and end up with cream sauce and cheese on top. Bake at 350° until bubbling hot. Combine this sauce with any pasta and sprinkle with Parmesan cheese. Why be in a rut, though, for pastas? At least change the shape. Try Mostaccioli for a change. This recipe would be enough for six or eight people. Serve a salad of greens and fennel with oil and vinegar dressing and a Caramel Orange for dessert.

Veal

Veal Kidneys in Cognac

(FOR TWO OR FOUR)

2 small veal kidneys	1 teaspoon lemon juice
¼ cup butter	1 tablespoon chopped
2 tablespoons cognac	parsley
¼ teaspoon dry mustard	

Salt and freshly ground pepper

Remove fat and membrane from the kidneys and slice very thin. Sauté quickly in butter. Add the cognac and light. Shake pan while you continue cooking until the brandy is reduced to ½ the original amount. Remove kidneys to heated platter, add the mustard, lemon juice and parsley to the remaining liquid. Return kidneys to sauce, season and serve at once. You have to be brave to serve kidneys, unless you are sure about its acceptance. However, kidneys prepared in this manner, will make new friends for yourself and the dish. Nice for a Sunday morning brunch, with Grits Soufflé — and Blueberry Coffee Cake.

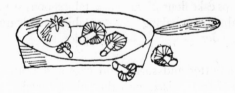

Grits Soufflé

2 cups milk
½ cup grits
1 teaspoon salt
½ teaspoon baking
   powder

½ teaspoon sugar
2 tablespoons melted
   butter
3 eggs, separated

Scald milk, add the grits and cook until thick. Add the salt, baking powder, sugar and butter. Beat the egg yolks and add to the grits mixture. Beat the egg whites to a soft peak and fold in the batter. Pour into a well buttered 1½-quart casserole and bake uncovered in a 375° oven for 25 to 30 minutes. Cornmeal may be substituted for the grits.

Blueberry Coffee Cake

(FOR 1 9-INCH CAKE PAN)

⅓ cup butter
⅓ cup sugar
2 eggs
¾ cup milk
1½ cups cake flour sifted
1 tablespoon baking
   powder

2 cups blueberries,
   fresh or frozen
1 3-ounce package
   cream cheese
2 tablespoons sugar
1 tablespoon lemon
   juice

Cream butter and sugar, add eggs and beat. Add milk and flour mixed with the baking powder. Add 1 cup of the blueberries and mix well. Pour into buttered 9-inch cake pan and sprinkle remaining berries on top. Mix the cheese with the sugar and lemon juice, and spread over top of berries. Place a crumb mixture on top and bake at 375° for 30 minutes. When done serve as is, or cover with a thin powdered sugar and water icing. Substitute any fruit for the berries.

CRUMB MIXTURE

1 cup cake flour   ¼ cup butter
¼ cup sugar   ¼ teaspoon cinnamon

Work together to make crumbs.

In France, the sauce to the meat is ceremony. One gets a feeling the French see Americans coming and say, "Give them the sauce." However, the French sauces are delicious, and all generously doused with wine. I must say I think veal dishes are better with a spot of wine added.

Veal à la Crème

(FOR SIX OR EIGHT)

1 teaspoon sugar	2 tablespoons butter
¼ cup sliced onion	2 tablespoons flour
3 pounds veal cut for stew	½ cup dry white wine
1½ cups chicken stock or water	½ cup whipping cream
	½ teaspoon grated lemon peel

Melt the sugar in a skillet casserole and brown onion in it. Add the meat and chicken stock (or water). Cover and simmer until fork-tender. Melt the butter, add the flour and stir in the wine and cream. Add salt if needed, then add to the veal with the lemon peel and cook 5 minutes. This is a delicately flavored dish, so the vegetables served with it should not overshadow it. Rice or noodles cooked in chicken stock, new potatoes, little white onions, baby zucchini with chives in the butter or fresh carrots would be good with it, but lightly seasoned. Again a chilled white wine would go well. For dessert, a combination of canned fruits sprinkled with brown sugar and butter and baked until hot. Run under broiler for the glisten you like.

This recipe for veal cutlets takes less than thirty minutes and is delicious. Good, too, for buffet suppers.

Veal and Mushrooms

(FOR SIX OR EIGHT)

2 pounds thinly sliced veal cutlets
½ cup butter or margarine
½ cup thinly sliced onion
½ pound fresh mushrooms sliced or 1 can of mushrooms (sliced)

1 tablespoon flour
1 cup cream
1 cup dry white wine (chicken consommé for those who do not like wine)
2 tablespoons chopped parsley

Cut the veal into 1-inch strips and sauté in the butter with the onion and mushrooms over low heat until brown. Blend the flour into mixture and stir until completely blended. Add the cream and simmer until tender, about 5 minutes. Add wine and parsley and season to taste. Simmer for 5 minutes. Leave out the cream if you like and add consommé. A bottle of chilled Chablis with it.

Asparagus or broccoli lightly buttered and sprinkled with toasted sesame seeds, and green or egg noodles are good with it. Fruit and cheese for dessert. Toast sesame seeds in a 300° oven.

Sweetbreads are good done this way too.

Meatballs for a gourmet dinner, for a cocktail tidbit, and especially for Potluck — and these have taken top priority for all meatballs.

Veal and Pork Meatballs

1½ pounds ground veal
¼ pound ground fresh pork
3 tablespoons butter
1½ hard rolls or 1½ slices dry bread
2 tablespoons grated onion
½ teaspoon grated lemon peel

3 eggs, beaten
½ teaspoon pepper
1 teaspoon salt
1 tablespoon lemon juice
1 teaspoon Worcestershire sauce
Chopped parsley
1½ quarts stock or bouillon

Mix meats with 2 tablespoons butter. Moisten rolls with water; when soft, squeeze water out and mix bread with meat. Cook onion in remaining butter until browned. Add to meat mixture with lemon peel, eggs, pepper, salt, lemon juice, Worcestershire, and parsley. Mix thoroughly. Shape in 12 balls (or 48 small ones for a cocktail tidbit). Heat bouillon or stock to boiling; drop balls in and simmer, covered, 15 minutes. Remove from stock with slotted spoon to a warmed dish and make

GRAVY

2 tablespoons butter
2 tablespoons flour
2 tablespoons chopped parsley

2 tablespoons capers
½ cup buttered crumbs
2 cups stock in which meatballs were cooked

Stir the butter and flour mixed together into hot

stock; cook and stir until smooth and boiling. **Add** parsley, capers and crumbs.

Serve the meat balls on noodles or with

Spaetzle

2¼ cups sifted flour
 1 egg, beaten

⅔ cup water
½ teaspoon salt

Mix into a soft dough. Form into a log about 2 inches in diameter; let stand 30 minutes. Slice thin and drop in boiling salted water.

Also serve spaetzle with a sauce made from mixing ¼ cup butter with ¼ cup sour cream. Heat in a skillet and drop the spaetzle in it. Shake over low heat until blended. Nice with roast beef.

I would probably serve a zany dessert like

Chocolate Stuffed Figs

2 pounds dried figs (large)
1 cup heavy cream
½ pound sweet chocolate

1 teaspoon rum
¼ pound semi-sweet chocolate
Candied violets

Slit a pocket in the figs. Heat the cream, add the sweet chocolate. Bring to a boil. Cool and stir until smooth and thick, add rum. Fill the figs and refrigerate. Melt the semi-sweet chocolate, dip half of fig in it and dry at room temperature. Roll candied violets to a dust and sprinkle over the chocolate. Serve these for a cocktail sweet bit, and start conversation.

Veal Cutlet Fontina

(FOR FOUR)

8 thin slices of veal
3 tablespoons butter
1 cup cream
¾ pound Fontina cheese

1 cup julienne of ham (Prosciutto if possible)
3 tablespoons Parmesan cheese

3 egg yolks

Dust the veal cutlets with seasoned flour and sauté in the butter until light brown. Mix rest of ingredients and cook in a double boiler until thick. Spoon over the veal, brown under the broiler and serve on noodles or rice, and I like

Saffron Rice

(FOR FOUR)

1 cup long-grained rice
1 tablespoon butter
1 tablespoon olive oil

2½ cups boiling chicken bouillon
¼ teaspoon saffron
¼ cup white wine

Salt and pepper

Brown rice in the butter and olive oil. Add the chicken bouillon, saffron and wine. Cover and cook over low heat until liquid is absorbed. Season with salt and pepper.

92

You do not have to go into a whirl over finding Fontina cheese. Use Bel Paese or Swiss Gruyère as a substitute.

Why would you want to dress salad greens with anything but olive oil and red wine vinegar for an entrée like this?

Melon Glory

For a quick and refreshing dessert (for four or six)

1 cup cubed water-
  melon
1 cup cubed canta-
  loupe
½ cup sliced straw-
  berries

1 sliced banana
1 cup fresh blueberries
  or raspberries

or any combination of fruit you would like. Place in a crystal bowl, cover with

2 tablespoons pow-
  dered sugar
½ cup Marsala wine

1 jigger of cherry
  brandy or your fa-
  vorite cordial

Refrigerate, and serve when you get around to it — today or tomorrow. If you do not like alcohol, cover with maple syrup and ice water — half and half.

Veal chops make a dinner fit for a king, especially when done with sour cream.

Veal Chops in Sour Cream

(FOR FOUR)

4 veal chops ½-inch
  thick or more
Salt and flour
¼ cup butter or
  margarine

1 cup sour cream
2 tablespoons lemon
  juice and finely
  slivered rind of
  1 lemon

Sprinkle the chops with salt and dredge them lightly in flour. Shake off all you can. Sauté lightly in butter for 15 minutes. Turn once. Add the sour cream to the skillet you cooked the chops in and cook over very low heat until the sauce is yellow. Add the lemon juice and rind and simmer a minute. Serve at once.

Green beans (fresh) cooked underdone and dressed with chopped dill and parsley are nice with it, and garlic potatoes.

Garlic Potatoes

16 small new potatoes
¼ cup melted butter
 1 garlic clove, crushed,
   or ½ teaspoon garlic
   salt

½ cup chopped parsley
 1 teaspoon salt

Boil potatoes covered for 5 minutes. Drain and sauté
in the butter until tender and golden. Shake frequently. Add the garlic, parsley and salt and serve at
once.

There is nothing more delightful to taste than sweetbreads for those who like them. For those who think
they do not, try a little positive thinking for a change.

Sweetbread Casserole

(FOR SIX)

2 pairs sweetbreads
½ lemon
¼ pound dried chipped
   beef
 1 cup sliced or canned
   B in B mushrooms

2 tablespoons butter
2 cups Thin Cream
   Sauce
Salt and pepper

Soak sweetbreads in cold water for 20 minutes.
Drain, cover with cold water to cover, add 1 teaspoon
salt, and juice of ½ lemon. Simmer for 30 minutes.
Make the sauce.

THIN CREAM SAUCE

2 tablespoons butter   ¼ teaspoon salt
1 tablespoon flour   1 cup milk

Melt butter in top part of double boiler, add flour and salt and cook until bubbly. Slowly add milk and stir briskly. Cook over hot water until thick and smooth, stirring occasionally.

Plunge sweetbreads into cold water. Remove skin and membranes. Slice or break into small (but not too small) pieces. Sauté the mushrooms in butter, add chipped beef and sweetbreads and cook for 5 minutes. Add cream sauce. Pour into buttered casserole, cover with ¼ cup bread crumbs, ¼ cup Parmesan cheese and dot with butter. Bake until crumbs are brown.

Since the beginning of time, sweetbreads have been served in cream sauce in a patty shell — but this version is good.

Sweetbreads with Madeira and Almonds

(FOR FOUR)

2 pairs sweetbreads, soaked, parboiled and skinned (see Sweetbread Casserole, p. 95)
2 tablespoons butter
½ cup almonds

½ cup Madeira
¼ cup sliced stuffed olives
2 cups medium cream sauce
Patty shells (buy them)
Paprika

Prepare sweetbreads and slice. Sauté in the butter with the almonds. Add the Madeira and continue cooking until reduced by one half. Add olives and cream sauce. Dip rims of patty shells in paprika and put in oven to heat. Serve the creamed mixture over them. Fingers of hot pineapple, baked in the oven with rum, brown sugar and butter sprinkled over, go well with them.

We in the Zodiac Room like to serve this over eggs deviled with minced ham added to the yolks, for a brunch, along with tomato halves baked and piled high with cooked frozen peas put through a Foley mill, seasoned with a pinch of nutmeg. We serve cinnamon bread sticks and hot biscuit and strawberry jam with them, and champagne glasses of fresh orange juice with a scoop of orange or pineapple ice in them.

Lamb

Lamb is a controversial subject, but not if you approach it with an open mind.

Lamb Stew

¼ cup diced onion
1 tablespoon butter
2 pounds lamb stew meat (shoulder is best, about 1-inch cubes)

1 teaspoon paprika
1 clove garlic, crushed
1 fresh tomato, peeled and chopped
1 can consommé
1 teaspoon salt

Arrowroot

In a heavy bottom skillet, brown onion in the butter till soft. Add stew meat rubbed with paprika. Add garlic and brown lightly. Add tomato and cook until soft. Add 1 can consommé and cook until tender. Add more consommé or water if necessary. Add salt, remove garlic. Thicken slightly with arrowroot.

Serve with hot, well-seasoned baby carrots, peas, new potatoes and mushrooms. I hope you all have discovered the Belgian carrots in the markets; that is, if you just will not prepare fresh ones. When I serve lamb stew to non-believers I add ¼ cup of hot bourbon, light it and stir in front of my guests. After their raves, I announce it is lamb and bourbon. I dash bourbon over lamb chops, too, and light. Amazing results.

Lamb needs a touch of mint most folks say, so why not in the salad. Mint by the way is good with any green salad.

½ cup olive oil
Juice of 1 lemon
  1 teaspoon ground
    fresh pepper

1 teaspoon chopped
  fresh mint
¼ teaspoon orégano
1 coddled egg

Combine in a bowl olive oil, lemon juice and seasonings. Add egg and whip. Pour over salad greens.

Or in the dessert —

Chocolate Mint Mousse

1 tablespoon gelatin
¼ cup water
  2 squares bitter chocolate
¼ cup water
  8 chocolate-covered
    mint wafers

⅔ cup sugar
1 cup milk, scalded
1¾ cups whipping
  cream
1 teaspoon vanilla

Soak gelatin in ¼ cup of water. Melt the chocolate with ¼ cup of water in top of double boiler. Add the mint wafers; blend thoroughly. Add the sugar and scalded milk; blend. Pour chocolate mixture over the gelatin; mix well. Cool until slightly thickened. Whip cream until thick and shiny. Add vanilla to slightly thickened gelatin mixture; fold in whipped cream. Pour into mold. Refrigerate until set, three hours or more. Unmold; arrange mounds of whipped cream around base. (Sprinkle chopped nuts over all, if desired.)

In educating less discriminating appetites to be discriminating, I stuff lamb shoulders and roast — and sell out!

Stuffed Lamb Shoulder

(FOR SIX OR EIGHT)

1 3- to 4-pound lamb shoulder, boned
1 cup finely chopped chicken livers, about ½ pound
¼ cup finely chopped mushroom stems
2 tablespoons butter
2 tablespoons chopped parsley
2 tablespoons finely chopped ham
Juice and grated peel of 1 lemon
1 egg yolk
Salt, pepper and paprika
½ teaspoon rosemary, crushed
½ cup dry white wine or water

Sauté the livers and mushroom stems in the butter until soft. Add parsley, ham, lemon juice and peel and egg yolk. This will be a coarse paste. Place in center of lamb, and roll, tie, or fasten with skewers. Rub with salt, pepper, paprika and rosemary. Roast uncovered at 300° for 2 hours or to the doneness you like and baste with the wine. Add more if you need it. Drain off excess fat and slightly thicken the juices with arrowroot, or serve au naturel. Good cold too!

Loin lamb chops are less expensive than rib as a rule.
Those people who do not like lamb like them this
way.

Lamb Chops à La Suisse

4 8-ounce loin lamb
  chops
Salt and pepper
½ cup chopped mush-
  rooms or stems
2 tablespoons butter

2 tablespoons sherry
4 thin slices Swiss cheese
  or Muenster, if you are
  the buy-it-already-
  sliced kind of cook

Broil seasoned chops under low heat about 10 minutes on each side. Place in a casserole or heat proof
platter. Sauté the mushrooms in the butter and
sherry. Pour over the chops. Cover with the cheese,
and run under the broiler. In fact you can cover up
many not-so-good-looking meat dishes by adding
Swiss or Muenster cheese on top and melting under
the broiler. Good for left over stew!

Pork

The young fry of today are the gourmets of to-morrow, and that goes for some of them right this minute. I am thrown for a recipe every so often for the under-twelve set, who are bored with the same old thing. Let's face this disinterest of theirs with foods that are different both in appearance and in taste.

Stuffed Pork Chops

3 strips bacon
2 tablespoons chopped onion
1 cup soft bread crumbs
1 cup peeled, chopped raw apple

¾ cup chopped cooked prunes
6 pork chops cut 1-inch thick
Salt, pepper and flour
½ cup pineapple juice
½ cup Sauterne

Mince bacon and cook until almost crisp. Add onion and cook 3 minutes (medium heat). Add crumbs, apples and prunes. Cut a slit in each chop and fill with the stuffing and fasten with a toothpick. Sprinkle with salt, pepper and flour. Brown in a heavy skillet, pour off fat and add the pineapple juice and wine. Cover and either bake at 325° or cook on top of the stove at low heat until tender, about 1 hour. Add more juice if necessary, or water. Serve with

Sweet Potatoes Marsala

4 medium sweet potatoes

½ cup butter
1 cup Marsala

Peel and cut the potatoes into fingers. Place in skillet with butter and wine; cover and simmer at low heat until done, and wine and butter is cooked into them.

A Chinese-inspired dinner goes a long way on a small food budget.

Sweet and Sour Pork

(FOR FOUR OR SIX)

1 tablespoon salad oil
2 pounds lean pork, sliced in thin strips
¼ green pepper cut in strips
2 slices canned pineapple cut in wedges
½ cup pineapple juice

1 cup chicken bouillon or water
2 teaspoons soy sauce
½ cup blanched whole almonds
¼ cup vinegar
¼ cup sugar
2 teaspoons cornstarch

¼ cup cold water

Heat the oil and add the pork slices. Brown in the oil at low heat. Cover and simmer for 10 minutes. Add the green pepper, pineapple, juice, bouillon, soy sauce, almonds, vinegar and sugar. Simmer for 5 minutes. Mix the cornstarch in the cold water and add. Cook until thickened. Substitute raw shrimp for the pork sometime.

Serve on hot rice. To go with it, snow peas, boiled covered for 1 minute, lightly buttered and seasoned with salt and pepper. Snow peas are in most of the markets today — pea pods for those not in the know!

108

Why not stay in the mood and serve

Chinese Almond Cookies
(ABOUT TWO DOZEN)

2 cups all-purpose flour	1 egg, beaten
½ teaspoon baking powder	½ teaspoon almond extract
1 cup butter or margarine	½ teaspoon vanilla extract
1 cup sugar	

2 dozen whole almonds, blanched

Sift flour and baking powder. Add butter, sugar and egg. Mix and knead until dough is firm. Roll out to ½-inch thickness. Cut with cookie cutter the desired size. Place an almond in center of each. Place 1½ inches apart on pan. Bake at 450° for 10 minutes, or until cookies begin to brown. Reduce to 250° and bake 20 minutes more.

Pork tenderloins lend themselves to wintry entertaining, and this recipe I particularly like.

Pork Tenderloin
(FOR FOUR)

2 2-pound pork tenderloins (1½ pounds is average weight)	¼ teaspoon rosemary (optional)
	¼ cup butter
Salt and pepper, dry mustard	½ cup currant jelly
	1 cup cream
2 tablespoons butter	1 tablespoon flour

109

Rub the tenderloins with salt, pepper and dry mustard, and brown in the 2 tablespoons of butter in a skillet. Sprinkle with rosemary (or skip it), the ¼ cup of butter and jelly. Cover and bake for 45 minutes in a 300° oven. Add the cream mixed with the flour and continue baking 15 minutes longer. Serve from the skillet or remove and place on a heated platter with rice and serve with the cream sauce. Just a green salad and an apple pudding would be sufficient. No doubt I would add corn sticks, which make a nice change.

Corn Sticks

(FOR TEN OR TWELVE)

2 cups water   1½ cups cornmeal
1¼ teaspoons salt
   1 cup grated sharp cheese

Bring the water and salt to boiling. Add cornmeal and mix thoroughly. Cook until the mixture separates from the sides and bottom of pan. Remove from fire, add cheese and mix. Take mixture out by teaspoonfuls and shape into balls. In the palms of the hands, roll balls to ½ inch thickness, in the shape of small cigars. Fry in hot deep fat (375°) for 2 or 3 minutes. Drain before serving.

Pork has an affinity for fruit and especially for citrus fruit.

Florida Pork Loin

(F O R   F O U R   O R   S I X)

1 3-pound piece of pork loin, boned or not (there is always more flavor if the bone is left in)
2 teaspoons salt

½ teaspoon Tabasco
¼ cup finely chopped onion
½ cup orange juice
½ cup water
1 lemon sliced thin

Cornstarch or arrowroot

Rub the pork with the salt and Tabasco. Place in a skillet with the onion and brown on both sides. Remove and pour off the fat, and return to skillet. Baste frequently with the orange juice and water, and bake uncovered for 2 hours at 300° or until done. Add the lemon slices on the top side the last 30 minutes. Drain off the excess fat and thicken the juices with a very little cornstarch or arrowroot — about ½ teaspoon to 1 cup of liquid.

Serve with thick slices of tomato baked until soft, and covered with mayonnaise flavored with garlic and run under the broiler, and broccoli undercooked and sprinkled with Parmesan cheese and poppyseeds — no butter is necessary. This pork is good cold also — and cold roast pork sandwiches made on raisin bread are terrific.

The smell of home cooking is always a welcome sign, especially on a cool night, and this one I like to do in a casserole.

Hawaiian Ham

(FOR FOUR OR SIX)

1 slice ham 2 inches thick
1 tablespoon honey
½ cup water
½ cup sugar
½ cup sherry
½ cup raisins
½ cup canned pineapple chunks

Place ham, honey and water in casserole and simmer on top of stove until water has evaporated. Add the rest of the ingredients. Cover and cook in a 325° oven until tender, about 1 hour. Remove cover and continue cooking until the sauce is transparent looking. Cut in thin slices and serve it with a corn soufflé — I like to do the soufflés in individual soufflé cups — then spill buttered peas over them. Same old thing, but they look pretty. Or you could bake it in a ring mold and fill the center with any green vegetable.

An American Brie cheese that is mighty good is produced in Lena, Illinois — Kalb brand. It is worth your investigation. It would make a nice ending for this meal with toasted unsalted crackers.

Entrées

I have a favorite dish for Friday or Sunday night called

Mushroom Rarebit

4 tablespoons butter
4 tablespoons flour
2 cups milk
2 cups canned mush-
room soup
1 teaspoon Worcester-
shire
4 drops Tabasco

½ teaspoon salt
12 whole mushrooms,
sautéed
1 cup sliced mush-
rooms, sautéed (you
can use B. in B.)
1 pound cheddar
cheese

¼ cup sherry

Make a cream sauce by melting the butter, adding the flour and cooking until bubbly. Add milk and cook until thick. Add rest of the ingredients. Mix and cook until smooth and hot. Spoon over toasted English muffins and pass sliced hard cooked eggs and slivered black olives to go with it.

For a sophisticated luncheon, any time of the year.

Mushrooms Paprika

(FOR TWO OR FOUR)

1 pound fresh mush-
rooms
¼ cup butter
2 tablespoons finely
chopped onion

¼ teaspoon salt
1 teaspoon paprika
1 tablespoon flour
¼ cup white wine
1 cup sour cream

Wash mushrooms, and peel if you wish, but it is not necessary. Sauté in the butter with the onion, salt, and paprika until done. Add the flour and cook 1 minute. Add wine, continue cooking, add sour cream. Bring to a boil, but do not let it boil.

Serve on melba toast, thinly buttered, with corn soufflé and cold asparagus with Vinaigrette sauce.

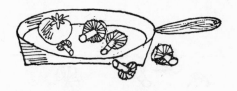

A popular Potluck luncheon is

Mushrooms and Artichokes
in Mustard Cream
(FOR FOUR)

8 large mushrooms
¼ cup butter
1 tablespoon flour
½ cup milk
½ cup light cream
1½ teaspoons prepared
mustard

1½ cups artichoke
hearts (canned or
frozen)
Pastry shells
1 tablespoon chopped
chives

Sauté the mushrooms in the butter until tender. Remove. Add the flour, cook until bubbly, and add the milk, cream and mustard. Cook until thick. Add the mushrooms and the artichokes heated in their juices. Serve on thin pastry shells with the chives sprinkled on top. Especially nice for a Friday luncheon — and you could use canned mushrooms if you wish, and serve from the skillet you prepare it in. With it — lemon buttered fresh okra and hot peeled cherry tomatoes and a

Fruit Ring
with Apricot Dressing

½ pound dried apricots
½ cup water

Simmer until tender. Remove and add ¼ cup sugar. Mix (in blender) until fruit is a pulp. Set aside ¼ cup for dressing.

2 packages Lime Jello
3½ cups hot water
1 cup canned crushed pineapple
½ cup slivered almonds
2 3-ounce packages cream cheese

1 cup whipping cream
1 tablespoon sherry
⅓ cup powdered sugar
¼ teaspoon vanilla
¼ teaspoon almond extract
Salad greens

Prepare Jello. Let cool and when it begins to congeal, add apricots, pineapple and almonds. Pour into salad mold. Let set in refrigerator. Beat cream cheese with the ¼ cup of mashed apricots, ¼ cup of cream and sherry until smooth and fluffy. Whip remaining cream, add sugar, flavorings and cream cheese mixture. If you like a thinner dressing, add more cream. This dressing is good on any fruit salad, congealed or otherwise.

This is a wonderful, simple, elegant Potluck. For an entrée or with chicken or duck.

Rice Salad

(F O R   S I X)

2 cups cooked chilled rice	1 tablespoon chopped chives
½ cup chopped king crab or lobster	¼ cup chopped parsley
½ cup slivered ham (Virginia if available)	1 tablespoon olive oil
½ cup finely chopped celery	1 tablespoon wine vinegar
2 finely chopped hard-cooked eggs	½ cup mayonnaise
	Salt
	Freshly ground pepper

Combine by tossing lightly the first seven ingredients. Sprinkle with oil and vinegar. Add mayonnaise and season. Let stand in refrigerator a few hours for still better flavor. This would have a way of finding itself at many buffet parties, I would plan. I served this to some guests who had most definite ideas about what they liked to eat, and they shuddered politely, if that is possible, at the thought of rice salad. They all came back for a big second helping. With it I had crisp roasted duck and Florentine tomatoes — and poached fresh peaches for dessert that I served from a large crystal compote. The color is beautiful! I also used fresh peaches for my centerpiece, piled on a brass compote, some cut in half to show the stone and varied color of the peach. I merely rubbed the halves with lemon juice to keep their color. I felt the party a success when my men guests asked to take a peach home for breakfast — and there went my centerpiece and my budget.

I get carried away with cheese dishes — but who doesn't like them? I have a frequent visitor to my home who says he dislikes cheese — but he eats my soufflés and custards with relish.

Cheese Custard

1 cup sour cream	½ teaspoon salt
½ cup grated Swiss cheese	3 egg yolks
	3 egg whites
¼ teaspoon paprika	½ teaspoon salt

2 tablespoons grated Parmesan cheese

Mix the cream, Swiss cheese, paprika, and salt. Add the egg yolks beaten until light. Pour into a buttered casserole and place in a pan of hot water. Bake at 375° for 20 minutes. Beat the egg whites until stiff, fold in salt and cheese. Pile on top of the custard and return to oven for 8 minutes or until meringue is brown. This I like to serve with a cold buffet as my one hot entrée. For instance:

Cold corn beef glazed with chutney
Cheese custard
Marinated green beans
Creamy coleslaw
Thin slices of assorted breads, buttered
Watermelon preserves
A bowl of ice cream with Rum Raisin Sauce

Rum Raisin Sauce

½ cup rum
½ cup seedless raisins
½ cup sugar
¼ cup water
1 stick cinnamon
(you may omit)
¼ teaspoon vanilla

1 tablespoon grated
lemon peel
1 tablespoon grated
orange peel
½ cup pecan pieces
(you may omit)

Pour rum over raisins and let stand until raisins are puffed. Mix sugar, water and cinnamon and boil 2 minutes. Discard cinnamon and add raisins and rum. Cook for 5 minutes. Add vanilla. Remove from heat and add lemon and orange peel. Add nuts and serve warm, over ice cream.

Everyone loves a soufflé, and why not? This one is easy, but must be eaten as soon as it is ready. It approaches the French soufflé in texture and appearance.

Cheese Soufflé

(FOUR SERVINGS)

4 tablespoons butter	1½ cups milk
4 tablespoons flour	½ pound Old English
1 teaspoon salt	process cheese,
Cayenne	grated

6 eggs, separated

Melt butter in top of double boiler. Blend in flour, adding salt and a few grains of cayenne. Add milk gradually, blending well. Heat to boiling point, cook, stirring constantly until the sauce is thick and smooth. Boil at least one minute after you think it is enough. Add cheese and continue cooking, stirring frequently, until cheese is melted. Remove from heat and slowly add beaten egg yolks, blending them in well. Let mixture cool. Start oven at slow (300°). Pour cooled cheese mixture into stiffly beaten egg whites, cutting and folding thoroughly together. Pour at once into ungreased casserole. Run tip of a teaspoon around the mixture 1 inch from edge of casserole, making a slight track, or depression. This forms the "top hat" on the soufflé as it bakes and puffs up. Bake in slow oven 1 hour and 15 minutes. Carry soufflé in baking dish to table and serve immediately. The straight sided French casserole is best for this, but not necessary. Be sure you cook your cream sauce until thick, then start counting. Use this to spoon creamed foods over for a change.

A good cheese torte can be the answer to many demands. It is extra special for a cocktail table where each guest may cut his own piece. It is the answer for Friday entertaining or just family. Most of all, I like it to "carry" creamed foods like chicken, seafood, leftover ham, chipped beef or just anything. Gets away from the toast bit, and the cheese flavor compliments any food. Save your scraps of cheese and make a real potluck taste. Even if it does not turn out perfect (and it should) it is still good.

Cheese Torte
(FOR SIX OR EIGHT)

4 egg yolks	⅛ teaspoon salt
1½ cups light cream or milk	⅛ teaspoon nutmeg
1½ cups grated Swiss cheese (or other)	4 egg whites

Beat egg yolks with the cream, add cheese, salt and nutmeg. Fold in egg whites stiffly beaten. Pour into an unbaked pie shell or pastry lined torte pan and bake at 350° for 30 minutes or until custard is set.

For an easy company luncheon, I would heat a cup of fresh crabmeat (or canned) with 2 tablespoons of butter, add ¼ cup of brandy, and light. Then add 1 cup of whipping cream and let simmer for 5 minutes. Pile it on top of the Torte, or spoon it over each pie-shaped piece when serving. Baby zucchini steamed and specially buttered, and Marsala carrots — same recipe as for Marsala Sweet Potatoes. After this array of flavors, thin slices of melon with a half lime for dessert.

123

Sauce for Vegetables

4 tablespoons butter
2 tablespoons bread
crumbs
⅛ teaspoon dry
mustard

1 tablespoon chopped
parsley
Grated rind of ½ lemon
1 teaspoon chopped
pimiento

Melt butter, add bread crumbs and brown with the dry mustard. Add parsley, pimiento, and lemon rind and let foam. Pour over or toss with any vegetable, but especially green.

Desserts

Ease in serving is more important today than time. What is easier or more gracious than serving Pots de Crème for dessert in the living room with coffee after dinner. The crème pots are available all over the country in china shops — so invest! Good too for holding vitamin pills, cocktail picks or whatever.

Pots de Crème

(FOR SIX)

6 egg yolks	⅛ teaspoon salt
½ cup sugar	1 teaspoon vanilla

2 cups coffee cream

Beat egg yolks until light and lemon-colored. Gradually beat in sugar and salt and vanilla. Stir in ¼ of the cream. Heat remaining cream and gradually stir into the egg mixture. Strain through a fine sieve into the crème pots or custard cups. Cover with the crème pot covers or foil if using custard cups. Set pots in a pan ¾ filled with water and bake. Bake at 325° for 1 hour, or until set. Chill before serving. You could put a teaspoon of caramelized sugar in the bottom of each pot before adding custard, or flavor them with dark rum — watch it!

CARAMELIZED SUGAR

1 teaspoon butter   ½ cup granulated sugar

Melt butter, add sugar and melt to a brown syrup. Add more sugar if you want more. Add water and stir to a thin syrup if you wish it thinner.

127

Crème de Cacao Cream

3 cups half milk and
cream
¾ cup sugar

9 egg yolks
4 tablespoons Crème
de Cacao

Scald cream with the sugar and cool slightly. Beat
egg yolks and add, stirring constantly. Add Crème de
Cacao. Set in a pan of water. Cover and bake at
350° for about 40 minutes or until a knife inserted
comes out clean. Serve very cold.

The most popular Potluck dessert we serve at N-M is Caramel Cup Custard. Old as the hills — but everyone loves it — young and old.

Caramel Cup Custard

(FOR FOUR OR SIX)

Mix well

⅓ cup sugar	3 whole eggs
Pinch of salt	½ cup light cream

Scald
 2 cups of milk
Add to egg mixture, whipping while you pour.

Add
½ teaspoon vanilla

In the meantime, put ½ cup of sugar in a heavy skillet and cook over medium heat, stirring constantly, until it is the color you desire. Add 1 tablespoon of water, and stir until completely blended.
   Put 1 tablespoon of the caramelized sugar into the bottom of the custard cups and pour the custard on top. Bake in a water bath at 350° until done (about 25 to 30 minutes).

A really elegant dessert is

Macaroon Stuffed Peaches

6 fresh, frozen or
canned peaches
1 dozen macaroons
(store bought)

1 yolk of egg
2 tablespoons sugar
¼ cup butter

If peaches are fresh, cut them in half, take out the stones and a little of the pulp to make a deep space for the stuffing. Crumble the macaroons and stir in the other ingredients. Stuff the peaches with this mixture, spreading it in a smooth mound over each half. Put them in a buttered fireproof dish and bake in a moderate (325°) oven for about 30 minutes.

Lime ice with canned mandarin oranges makes a low-in-calorie-looking dessert. Sprinkled with Cointreau, better still, and pretty for holiday time sprinkled with pomegranate seeds.

130

A dessert or even an accompaniment for meats of all kinds.

Apple Compote

2 cups sugar   2 cups water
                    ½ lemon, sliced

Boil for 5 minutes, add peeled and quartered

4 Rome Beauty or   1 cup of raisins that have
   Winesap apples   soaked in sherry for a
8 cooked prunes   few hours

Cook until the syrup is clear and the apples soft.
Serve hot or cold, with or without cream.

Caramel Orange

4 oranges   1 cup sugar
                  ½ cup water

Peel two of the oranges with a potato peeler (it's easier). Take the thin peelings of the 2 oranges, cut in thin strips, and drop in boiling water to rid them of the bitter taste. Then peel these oranges and the other two until no white is left on them. Run a sharp knife along each section of orange but do not remove the sections. Drop the whole orange in the boiling sugar and water and leave for 3 minutes. Remove the oranges and cool. Add the orange strips to the syrup left in the skillet and cook until they have a transparent look — and pour over the oranges. It is a beautiful and delicious dessert. Add a little Grand Marnier too if you like.

Apple Pudding

(FOR FOUR OR SIX)

2 eggs
¼ teaspoon salt
1 cup sugar
2 tablespoons plus 2
   teaspoons flour
1½ teaspoons baking
   powder

½ cup chopped pecans
   or walnuts
½ teaspoon vanilla
2 fresh Rome Beauty
   or Winesap apples,
   pared, cored and
   sliced

132

Beat eggs and salt together until light. Add rest of ingredients, mix and bake in a buttered casserole for 35 minutes at 375°. Really good with lemon ice cream on top or lemon flavored whipped cream, but neither is necessary.

Ice Cream Whip would be good to keep on hand all year long, as everyone will love it.

Ice Cream Whip

(FOR SIX OR EIGHT)

1 quart strawberries or raspberries
Juice of 1 lemon
3 tablespoons sugar
1 cup chopped pecans
1 cup chopped pistachio nuts
½ cup confectioner's sugar
3 cups whipped cream

Mash the berries with the lemon juice and sugar. Let stand ½ hour. Add nuts and confectioner's sugar and stir. Fold in the whipped cream. Pour into loaf pans or an ice cream mold and freeze in your freezing compartment. Slice and serve. Or substitute peaches for the berries and almonds for the pecans but keep the flavor of the pistachio.

133

Strawberry Cream Custard

(FOR SIX OR EIGHT)

4 egg yolks	2 cups heavy cream
2 tablespoons sugar	1 quart fresh straw-
1½ cups milk	berries
Piece of vanilla bean	½ cup Kirsch

½ cup powdered sugar

Combine the first four ingredients in the top of a double boiler and cook over hot water, stirring from time to time, until the custard coats the spoon. Discard the vanilla bean. Cool the custard and fold in the cream, whipped stiff. Chill the mixture in the refrigerator. Clean the berries and sprinkle them with sugar and the Kirsch. Chill in the refrigerator for 1 hour. Gently blend the two mixtures and refrigerate for 1 hour or more before serving.

The smell of cinnamon goes through the house with

Baked Bananas

2 tablespoons butter	2 tablespoons light
4 bananas	brown sugar

1 teaspoon cinnamon

Melt the butter in a skillet. Add the peeled bananas whole or split (lengthwise). Mix sugar and cinnamon. Sprinkle with half the sugar and cinnamon and sauté until light brown. Turn and sprinkle with rest of the sugar and cinnamon. Serve warm for dessert or with ham or chicken. Be daring! Add 2 jiggers of rum and ignite.

Even canned applesauce, thinned down with maraschino cherry juice and spooned over lemon or orange sherbet, is a pretty and delicious dessert, and lower in calories.

If you are feeling gay but lazy, serve a Velvet Hammer, a specialty of many a good restaurant for an after dinner drink — but a wonderful dessert. This is my version.

Velvet Hammer

1 pint vanilla ice
   cream
2 jiggers brandy

1 jigger cointreau
1 jigger crème de cacao
   (white)

Put in your blender, or whip with an eggbeater. Serve at once in stemmed glasses. For 2 or 4, depending on your generosity.

A good frozen pudding to have on hand all the year round, and especially at holiday time. It would be a good idea to have this in your deep freeze for any occasion that calls for dessert, during the holidays — or why the holidays? — any day!

Frozen Holiday Pudding

1 pint pistachio ice cream	Store-bought pound cake or make your own
1 pint strawberry ice cream	Kirsch
	Crème de cacao
1 pint vanilla ice cream	Cointreau
1 pint coffee ice cream	Brandy

or any combination of ice creams
and liqueurs you like best.

Cut the cake in ¼-inch slices to fit a loaf pan. Soak each slice in a different liqueur. Pack thin layer of pistachio ice cream in bottom of the pan, then place a slice of the soaked cake. Alternate the ice cream and slices of cake until the pan is full, the ice cream layer on top. Return to the deep freeze and leave for at least two days. Slice and serve on chilled plates. Neither the cake nor the ice cream should be more than ¼ inch thick, and the more layers of each you have the better the pudding. You can make it without the liqueur and have good results too.

You will like apples baked in cream for dessert, and be sure to serve warm or hot.

Apples in Cream

6 Rome Beauty or
   Winesap apples
4 tablespoons butter

6 tablespoons brown
   sugar
¾ cup heavy cream

Peel, core and quarter the apples and place in a shallow baking dish. Dot with butter and sprinkle the sugar over. Bake for 20 minutes at 325°, covered. Pour over the cream. Bake at 350° for 15 or 20 minutes, or until soft.

Glazed Peaches with Almonds

1 can peach halves (6)
½ cup slivered almonds
2 tablespoons brown
   sugar or honey

2 tablespoons lemon
   juice
½ teaspoon grated
   lemon rind

1 tablespoon butter

Place the peach halves in a casserole dish, round side down. Sprinkle with the almonds and sugar. Boil the juice from the fruit until reduced to 1 cup. Remove from fire, add the lemon juice and rind. Pour over the peaches, dot with butter and bake at 325° for 30 minutes. Serve hot or cold, with or without cream or ice cream.

Do not be afraid of

Grand Marnier Soufflé

(FOR SIX)

2 tablespoons butter	½ teaspoon vanilla
1½ tablespoons flour	5 egg yolks
½ cup scalded milk	4 tablespoons sugar
6 egg whites	

Melt butter, add flour and cook until golden. Add scalded milk and cook until thick. Cook 5 minutes stirring constantly. Add vanilla. Beat egg yolks with 3 tablespoons sugar and combine with the cream sauce. Beat 6 egg whites stiff, add 1 tablespoon sugar. Fold in half the egg whites, then the other half. Pour into a buttered and slightly sugared casserole. Bake at 400° for 20 minutes. Serve with 2 tablespoons of Grand Marnier added to 2 tablespoons whipped cream or pour over lighted Grand Marnier, or both.

An elegant dessert:

Poached Fresh Pears with Gingered Cream

½ cup sugar	1 sliced lemon
1 cup water	Pinch of salt
6 peeled fresh pears or peaches, apples and such	1 cinnamon stick

138

Bring sugar and water to a boil. Add fruit, lemon, salt and cinnamon stick. Simmer at medium heat until fruit is fork-tender. Remove to a bowl or serving dish. Serve with gingered cream.

GINGERED CREAM

1 3-ounce package cream cheese	2 tablespoons candied ginger, chopped fine
1 teaspoon lemon juice	2 teaspoons grated
1 cup whipping cream	orange peel

Finely chopped pistachio nuts

Mash cheese with lemon juice and cream and whip with beater or in an electric blender. Add ginger and orange peel and whip until well blended. Sprinkle nuts on top when serving. We also put it in a scooped-out orange half and serve with fresh fruit.

Here are some quickie desserts:

Drained canned pears, mixed with marrons and marron syrup and icy cold. For 1 can of each, heat ¼ cup of brandy, light and pour over the fruit. While it is still burning serve over coffee ice cream.

Glazed Fruit

6 fresh ripe peaches peeled and sliced	3 bananas, sliced
6 slices fresh pineapple, large dice	1 glass raspberry jelly Strawberries or raspberries

Arrange cold fruit in serving bowl. Melt jelly and pour over fruit. Top with berries. Serve on crystal plates.

Sherry Peaches

⅓ cup butter
¾ cup brown sugar
⅓ cup water

1 teaspoon lemon juice
6 large ripe peaches, skinned

½ cup sherry

Melt butter and sugar in a casserole; add water, lemon juice and whole peaches. Poach peaches slowly, being sure to baste them frequently with syrup. Depending on size of peaches, it takes from 20 to 30 minutes to cook. Add sherry in last 5 minutes of cooking. Serve hot with meats, or warm with cream for dessert.

Pancakes have become a national institution. I use thin rolled ones in place of vegetables with meats, for example — orange pancakes with chicken, lemon pancakes with lamb, blueberry with ham and so on. Try it!

Pancakes

1½ cups milk for thin ones, ¾ cup for thick ones

3 tablespoons melted butter

2 eggs, whites beaten separately

¾ teaspoon salt

3 tablespoons sugar

2½ teaspoons baking powder

1½ cups all-purpose flour, sifted

Have milk at room temperature and add with butter to egg yolks. Add dry ingredients sifted together and stir vigorously, adding more milk, if necessary, to make batter just thin enough to pour. Do not overbeat: lumps do no harm. Fold in beaten egg whites.

Orange Butter

1 cup powdered sugar   ¼ cup butter
Juice and grated rind of 1 orange

Whip together until light. Roll in pancake. Substitute lemon for the orange. When I use blueberries, I add them to the pancakes then use lemon butter — and thickened blueberry sauce on top — or buy blueberry syrup.

I have many choice hot fruits in my recipe file, but I find curried pears just go with anything from lamb to lobster.

Curried Pears

6 fresh pears (or
   12 canned halves)
½ cup butter

½ cup brown sugar
1 tablespoon curry
   powder
½ teaspoon salt

Peel, cut in half and remove core from pears. Mix and pile rest of ingredients in the cavities. Bake covered at 325° until soft. Remove cover and run under broiler until sizzling. A fruit plate made of an assortment of canned fruits prepared the same is a nice change for morning coffee or brunch.

Pasta
and Vegetables

Many of my Potluck vegetables are Italy-inspired. Why not? Italy is a relaxing place to be. Casserole vegetable dishes make you feel relaxed before and after eating them.

This is my favorite pasta dish. I use it as an entrée, as a vegetable and as a carrier for various seafoods in cream. As a buffet casserole it has no equal. One gal's opinion!

Tonnarelli

(FOR FOUR)

½ pound package very fine egg noodles
½ cup slivered left over ham — you may omit too

1 4-ounce can mushrooms or 1 pound fresh
3 tablespoons butter
1 cup cooked peas
½ cup Parmesan cheese

Cook noodles until tender. Drain but do not wash. Slice the mushrooms; if fresh, sauté in butter. Add to the hot noodles with butter, ham, peas and the cheese, and toss until everything is well coated with the cheese. I have had guests ask if there were leftovers to take home — so it must be good.

A very simple pasta to serve with anything you choose — or eat it alone with a glass of good red wine.

Ricotta Pasta

⅔ cup ricotta (or
   cottage cheese)
½ cup grated Parmesan
   cheese

A pinch of nutmeg
1 8-ounce package
   macaroni or any pasta
2 tablespoons butter

Salt and freshly ground black pepper

Mash the cheeses together, add the seasonings. Cook the pasta in boiling salted water, and place in a *hot* buttered serving casserole. Stir the cheese mixture into it. Add the butter, and place in a 350° oven for 5 minutes. Nice with broiled chicken. There is a pasta called Wagon Wheels — do it this way for a fun dinner.

I am an eggplant fan — especially eggplant in a casserole.

Eggplant Parmesan

(FOR FOUR OR SIX)

1 large eggplant	6 slices bacon
2 cups white bread cubes (no crust)	4 eggs
	1 cup milk
1 cup grated sharp cheese	1 tablespoon butter
	¼ cup Parmesan cheese

Peel and dice eggplant. Parboil in boiling salted water. Drain. Mix with the bread cubes, cheese and bacon (diced and the fat rendered out). Beat the eggs, add the milk and combine with the eggplant mixture. Pour into buttered 3-quart casserole; dot with butter and sprinkle with Parmesan cheese. Bake at 325° until set and brown.

Eggplant Italienne

1 large eggplant	1 teaspoon salt
Cooking oil	½ teaspoon pepper
1 #2 can tomatoes	½ teaspoon basil
2 cups sliced onion	¼ teaspoon orégano
1 clove garlic, minced	Dash of cayenne

¼ cup grated Parmesan cheese

Pare eggplant and cut into 2-inch cubes. Sauté slowly in oil in skillet, preferably iron, until lightly browned. Keep stirring so cubes don't burn or stick. Put tomatoes, onion, garlic and seasonings in saucepan and simmer slowly 20 minutes. Pour sautéed eggplant into a buttered casserole, pour tomato mixture over it, and sprinkle top generously with Parmesan cheese. Bake at 350° for 30 minutes.

The magic of vegetables lies in their dressing. Read with your taste buds for a change.

Cooked new potatoes tossed in a skillet with butter, lemon juice and grated lemon peel. Add to this chopped olives or parsley or onion flakes, or a little sour cream.

Add chopped leftover bits of ham and Roquefort cheese to mashed potatoes and casserole them. Bake at 350° until hot. Add to stuffed potato mixture too!

Croutons you make yourself, browned in butter with a pinch of curry powder or orégano, tossed into just undercooked green beans, or over asparagus or broccoli.

Some other special vegetables —

Red Beans and Rice

½ cup diced onion
¼ cup diced green
 pepper
2 tablespoons butter

3 cups canned or
 cooked red beans
1 cup diced leftover
 cooked ham
Rice

Sauté onion and green pepper in butter until soft. Add beans and ham. Pour into casserole and bake at 325° for 30 minutes. Serve with a scoop of rice.

Fried Plantains

Cut peeled plantains in diagonal slices, roll in flour
and sugar (1 teaspoon sugar to 1 cup flour). Brown
in a skillet with butter. A nice change from potatoes.

Gnocchi

2 cups mashed
   potatoes (left over)
1½ tablespoons flour

1 egg
½ cup grated Parmesan
   cheese

Mix and knead to a smooth paste. Make into small
balls, flatten, and roll lightly in flour. Drop in boiling water or stock. Serve with melted butter and
Parmesan cheese sprinkled over.

Use fried eggplant in place of toast to carry whatever
you wish to carry on it. Peel and slice as thin as you
possibly can. Drain in a colander for 1 hour. Sprinkle with salt and pepper and roll in flour lightly.
Sauté at medium heat in olive oil until brown. Turn
only once.

Limping Susan

¼ cup finely diced salt
  pork
1 cup rice
1 onion chopped fine
3 cups chicken broth
  or consommé

2 cups mashed canned
  tomatoes
2 tablespoons chopped
  parsley
Salt and pepper
Cooked okra

Slivers of cooked chicken

Fry pork until crisp. Add rice and stir until rice is golden. Add onion and cook until soft. Add broth (or water). Cover and cook until rice is done, about 1 hour. Add tomatoes and parsley and seasonings — fork-stir and bake uncovered for 30 minutes. Just before serving add cooked okra and slivers of leftover chicken or not.

Stuffed Mushrooms

1 cup ground leftover
  baked ham
Slivers of garlic,
  chopped

1 cup chopped parsley
1 cup chopped mush-
  room stems (sautéed)
2 cups bread crumbs

1 cup grated Parmesan cheese

Mix and stuff 24 large partially cooked fresh mushrooms. Sprinkle with olive oil and bake at 325° until hot.

151

Florentine Tomato

(FOR FOUR OR EIGHT)

4 tomatoes
1 package frozen
  spinach or 1½ pounds
  fresh
1 tablespoon chopped
  onion

1 tablespoon butter
Salt and pepper
Pinch of nutmeg
Parmesan cheese

Cut tomatoes in half and place in a 325° oven in a buttered casserole for 10 minutes. Heat spinach and onion only until ice is melted, or until leaves are wilted if using fresh. Drain. Put in electric blender, or chop fine. Mix with the butter, salt, pepper and nutmeg. Cook until hot. Pile on top of the tomato halves. Sprinkle generously with the cheese and put back in the oven for 10 minutes.

Celery Amandine

4 canned celery hearts
2 tablespoons butter
1 cup canned consommé
1 teaspoon arrowroot or
   cornstarch
2 tablespoons cold
   water

Salt and freshly ground
   pepper
½ cup slivered natural
   almonds (I like these
   browned in butter)
2 tablespoons chopped
   parsley

Brown the celery in the butter. Add the consommé and simmer for 5 minutes. Add the arrowroot or cornstarch to the cold water and add to the casserole. Cook until thickened. Season to taste. Sprinkle nuts on the top and run under broiler for 1 minute. Sprinkle with parsley. Divine! And especially good with beef.

Other celery combinations I like:

Fresh celery cut slant-wise and thin, boiled 1 minute only in salted water, then combined with salted peanuts or pecans and whipping cream or a thin cream sauce, or combined with sliced sautéed mushrooms and browned almonds, or dressed with sweet butter and lots of chopped parsley.

153

Onions — even canned, are a casserole standby.

Glazed Onions

(FOR SIX OR EIGHT)

2 cans little white   1 can beef consommé
  onions   4 tablespoons butter
       2 tablespoons brown sugar

Drain onions and place in buttered casserole. Flip
them around on high heat until they begin to get
brown. Pour over the consommé, butter and sugar.
Bake at 350° for 45 minutes.

Corn Pudding

(FOR EIGHT)

¼ cup butter   1¾ cups milk
¼ cup flour   3 cups fresh or frozen
2 teaspoons salt   corn, chopped (use
1½ tablespoons sugar   an electric blender)

3 eggs

Melt butter in saucepan, stir in flour, salt, and sugar.
Cook until bubbly, add milk and cook until thick.
Stir in the corn, either chopped or whole, but
chopped makes a smoother pudding. Stir in the eggs
that have been beaten until frothy. Pour into a well-
buttered casserole and bake in a hot water bath at
350° about 45 minutes. For a soufflé — fold in egg
whites separately.

Some More of
This and That

Package bought bread sticks can become a gourmet's delight, by rolling in melted butter, then in Parmesan cheese, or a mixture of sugar and cinnamon (1 cup sugar to ¼ cup cinnamon), or in orégano and paprika. Place in a 375° oven and heat. Be sure to roll in butter first or your idea will roll away too.

Pie Crust

4 cups sifted all-purpose flour, 2 teaspoons salt, 1⅓ cups shortening (and pure lard always makes the best), 2 tablespoons vinegar, approximately ¾ cup water. Cut shortening into the flour and salt, add vinegar and water. Mix lightly. Roll out to a thin crust. Do many ahead of time and freeze with wax paper or foil between.

Beef au Poivre

1 rib eye of beef, ¾ cup peppercorns, olive oil, salt, Burgundy wine. Rub rib eye or another boneless cut with olive oil and salt. Rub freshly ground or cracked pepper over the entire piece and roast in a 350° oven, about 20 minutes for each pound. Dash a cup of Burgundy wine over after the first hour, and baste with it frequently. Serve medium rare or rare for best-tasting results. Wonderful for a cocktail buffet! — with thin sliced French bread and sweet butter.

Top a casserole of mashed potatoes with thick sour cream, and brown in the oven.

Chicken Broth à la Zodiac

1 4-5-pound hen, 1 stalk celery, few sprigs of parsley, 1 small onion, 1 small carrot, water to cover, 1 tablespoon salt. Put into a deep kettle and simmer for several hours. You may add 6 cloves, 1 bay leaf, 1 sprig thyme, put in a tea caddy and leave in the kettle for 30 minutes — but we do not. Simmer until hen is ready to fall off the bones. Remove hen, strain and serve or break two eggs into the pot. Bring to a fast boil. Set aside until egg floats on top. Strain through a fine sieve or through cheese cloth. This for a clearer broth.

Party Chicken Salad

1 quart diced chicken or turkey, ½ cup finely diced celery, ½ cup finely diced apple, ½ cup seedless grapes, 1 banana, sliced, 2 cups mayonnaise, 1 teaspoon curry powder, ¼ cup whipping cream, salt to your taste. Mix lightly. Place in ring fashion on a bed of salad greens that have been dipped in paprika. Decorate with pomegranate seeds and kumquats. Use as a make-your-own tidbit with thin slices of bread surrounding the salad in place of the lettuce.

Sprinkle muffins with equal parts of cinnamon and sugar before baking. These would make children ask for more, and husbands too.

Leftover cooked vegetables make good sandwiches. Add enough mayonnaise to "stick 'em," and flavor with curry powder. Also a good way to use them up is to toss them all together, with cooked rice or noodles, and add a little grated lemon peel to revitalize them.

A really good marmalade: 2 cups canned apricots, 2 cups orange rind put through coarse grinder or electric blender, 4 cups sugar. Boil and drain oranges three times to remove bitterness. Put all ingredients in a heavy-bottomed pot and cook until the apricots have disappeared (as apricots).

Frozen artichokes, cooked, then covered with ½ cup sour cream and an equal amount of dehydrated soup mix makes an interesting vegetable.

Make rosemary a must on your kitchen shelf. Crush the leaves and sprinkle them on any meat or poultry before roasting. Add it to your hot biscuit recipe, sprinkle it in soup.

Mix cranberry sauce or relish with sour cream and add horseradish sauce, enough to know it is there. A wonderful change for turkey and such.

Grate carrots, cabbage and celery and add to sour cream. Heat it (not boiling) and use as a dip for a change.

Instant coffee may be added to any cake recipe, its icing also, for a flavor change. To custard, cream fillings, whipped cream — or sprinkle it on top of vanilla ice cream. Really it is the best way to use it. Try it in your Christmas Egg Nog.

For those who watch their calories and their cholesterol, there is a skillet called T-Fal. No butter or oil is necessary, and you can use it for many things. You must use low heat so there are never any burned places to scour. In fact you just rinse and wipe with a soft towel. You will begin to enjoy the real taste of meats cooked this way.

Add a bit of curry to sauces for any ham dish. It has amazing taste results.

To divide an egg — beat then measure.

Rinse the pan in cold water before scalding milk, to prevent sticking.

No ham but baked ham should go into a ham sandwich, and slice it paper thin. Pile as thick as you like, but slice it thin.

Creamed chestnuts with spinach soufflé could be called the hospitality vegetable of the South.

Sherbet Punch: 2 quarts gingerale, 1 quart sherbet (pineapple or orange best) will serve 20 people.

Regardless of how you serve it — fresh caviar costs from $37.50 up a pound.

160

Bananas in their skins should never be refrigerated. Avocados likewise. Dip slices of either in canned pineapple juice to prevent darkening if cutting a couple of hours in advance — or grapefruit, lemon, lime or orange juice.

Too many bites of food to pick up before dinner helps conversation but ruins the dinner.

Cut a pineapple in half lengthwise, scoop out meat. Fill half full with cooked rice, and fill with curried seafood or chicken. Cover spines of pineapple with foil, then bake the whole works in a 350° oven until hot. Remove the foil, decorate spines with flowers — and you have a beautiful entree — but do not serve hot food in a cold pineapple. It tastes just like that!

Double in brass with a pineapple. Cut off the top of a large pineapple. Scoop out the center. Fill with cut up fresh fruit. Put cover back on. Cover entire surface with blossoms, fastening with plastic toothpicks. Use it as a centerpiece and as dessert. Refrigerate until ready to use. Add appropriate liqueur to fruit if you wish.

2 cups of butter equals 1 pound — 1 stick of butter equals ½ cup or ¼ pound.

1 cup cottage cheese equals ½ pound. In searching for lower in calorie good tasting soups, add 1 cup cottage cheese to 1 can cream of tomato soup and heat.

½ pound American cheese equals 2 cups grated cheese. For lazy housewives and small kitchens — you may buy it already grated now.

Buy almond macaroons, and put together with chocolate icing. Nice for the sweet of a cocktail party.

Make macaroons yourself. 4 egg whites, 1 cup sugar, 1 cup almond paste (buy it), a few drops of almond extract. Beat egg whites until they form soft peaks. Add sugar and continue beating. Beat the almond paste, and add egg whites gradually. Add extract. Drop by teaspoons on a baking sheet lined with unglazed paper. Sprinkle lightly with sugar. Bake at 400° for 15 minutes. Remove at once from paper. Decorate with a half blanched almond before baking if you wish.

Use beer in place of milk for fritter batter. Blend together: 1½ cups beer, 1 cup flour, ¼ teaspoon salt, ¼ teaspoon Ac'cent.

Use cider for poaching white fish of any kind. A nice comfortable flavor!

Wrap a thin slice of Prosciutto (Italian ham) around a peeled fresh fig for a cocktail buffet item.

Scurry around and find fennel in the fresh vegetable markets. Slice it raw for a salad, boil it and dress with butter and Parmesan cheese for a change in vegetable taste.

If you really want to go "way out" for color, serve Red Velvet Cake: 1½ cups sugar, ½ cup shortening (Crisco), 2 eggs, 2 cups flour, 1 teaspoon salt, 1 tablespoon cocoa, 1 cup buttermilk, 2 ounces red coloring, 1 teaspoon vanilla, 1 teaspoon soda *in* 1 tablespoon vinegar. Cream sugar and shortening, add eggs and beat well. Sift flour, salt and cocoa three times and add alternately to creamed mixture with buttermilk. Add vanilla and coloring. Then *fold* in soda and vinegar but do not beat. Bake in two 9-inch pans at 350° for about 25 or 30 minutes. Frosting: 1 cup milk, 1 cup sugar, ¼ teaspoon salt, ¼ cup flour, 1 cup butter (or margarine), 2 teaspoons vanilla, 1 cup Angel Flake Coconut. Mix flour and salt with milk until blended, cook slowly until real thick. Cool thoroughly. Cream butter and sugar until fluffy, then add to cooled mixture and beat well. (It looks like whipped cream.) Put on cake and garnish with coconut.

Who isn't tired of the same old chiffon pies? Give them a new lease on life by serving with a sauce, for instance, lemon soft custard over strawberry, puréed strawberries (electric blender) over lemon. Follow the same idea with the same ole cream pies.

Melt semi-sweet chocolate and pour over baked crusts to make a lining before adding the filling — as, Orange Chiffon Pie in a chocolate lined crust.

½ pint of heavy cream makes 2 cups of whipped cream.

A quick cocktail snack — junior size shredded wheat, garlic or plain buttered, browned in a 375° oven.

Two Phoenicians, Selech and Misor, taught man the art of heightening the flavor of food by mixing with

163

it a certain quantity of salt. The science of seasoning has no other origin.

Esau, pressed by hunger, sold his birthright to Jacob
for a dish of lentils.

About 1 medium avocado put in your electric
blender with 1 teaspoon lemon juice, then stirred
into 1 quart of softened vanilla ice cream makes a
beautiful and provocative tasting dessert. Nice to
spoon over fresh fruit too.

Broiled canned cling peaches go well with anything,
and help to satisfy the urge for something sweet.
Sprinkle with cinnamon and sugar beforehand, still
better, and with catsup — especially with lamb or
ham.

Serve tiny hamburgers sautéed in claret for a cocktail
bit. Place a hot smoked oyster on top!

You may add thinly sliced black olives to any
creamed dish to change its taste and appearance. It
also makes a guest think you are extravagant.

If you must go the easy route for hot hors d'oeuvres
combine canned meat balls, baby franks, button
mushrooms and pitted ripe olives. Sauté in butter
with a spot of sherry. Season well and keep hot in a
chafing dish. At least your guests have a choice.

The cackling of hens infallibly announced among
the ancients some dreadful calamity to the person
who had the misfortune to hear it, so they fattened
the hens for eating.

164

In the sixteenth century a Bishop of Paris was authorized by a bull from Pope Julius III, to permit the use of eggs during Lent. The Parliament took offense and prevented the execution of the mandate. From this severe abstinence from eggs during Lent arose the custom of having a great number of them blessed on Easter Eve, to be distributed among friends on Easter Sunday.

Fruit Luncheon Salad

1 package Lime Jello
¼ cup pineapple juice
1 3-ounce package
  cream cheese
½ cup marshmallows,
  cut up

¼ cup slivered almonds
1 cup crushed
  pineapple
¼ cup mayonnaise
1 cup cream, whipped

Dissolve Jello in ¼ cup pineapple juice. Add ¾ cup boiling water, cream cheese and marshmallows. When dissolved, add rest of ingredients. Fold whipped cream in when other ingredients begin to congeal. (Royal Ann cherries may also be added.) Makes 12 individual molds.

Buffet Corned Beef

4 pounds Beef Brisket
2 sliced oranges
1 sliced lemon
2 peeled onions, sliced

¼ cup brown sugar
1 tablespoon pickling
  spices

Cover beef with cold water, bring to a boil and skim. Add the fruit, sugar and spices. Simmer until tender, about 4 hours. Remove, sprinkle with brown sugar and bake at 350 degrees until sugar melts.

Apple Casserole

1½ cups sugar
2 quarts quartered
  apples

½ pound butter
Pie crust

Sprinkle a little sugar in bottom of casserole. Melt
over direct heat until brown. Pile apples in, add the
butter and sugar. Cover with pie crust and bake
until apples are soft at 375°. Serve cold with hot
caramelized sugar poured over.

A Holiday Relish Bowl

Whole cherry tomatoes, well washed, and crisped
raw brussel sprouts, pickled okra, whole tiny beets,
with a dip that might go like this:

1 3-ounce package
  cream cheese
1 cup sour cream

2 tablespoons horse-
  radish sauce
¼ cup chopped parsley

½ teaspoon onion juice

Leave the cream cheese out of the refrigerator to
soften. Whip and fold into the sour cream. Add
rest of ingredients and chill.

A gift of a SUGARED FRUIT RING would be a
nice neighborly gesture, and certainly a nice change
for your Christmas centerpiece. You can "sugar" any
fruit, and arrange as you see fit. Dip the fruit in egg
white, unbeaten, and roll in granulated sugar. Let
dry and arrange.

Index

Index

169

172

176

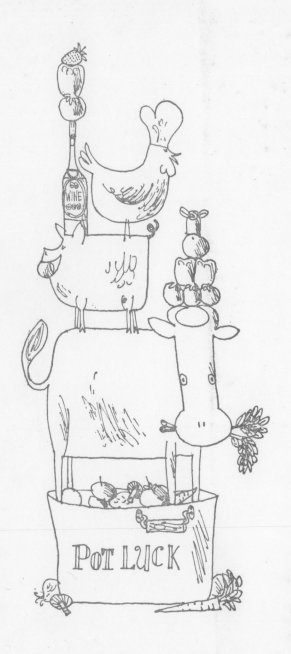

POT LUCK